UNCOMMON HAPPINESS

Rangjung Yeshe Books • www.rangjung.com

Padmasambhava: *Treasures from Juniper Ridge* • *Advice from the Lotus-Born* •
Dakini Teachings • *Following in Your Footsteps: The Lotus-Born Guru in Nepal*
• *Following in Your Footsteps: The Lotus-Born Guru in India* • *Followig in
Your Footsteps: The Lous-Born in Tibet, Vol. 3*

Padmasambhava and Jamgön Kongtrül: *The Light of Wisdom, Vol. 1, Vol. 2,
Vol. 3, Secret, Vol. 4 & Vol. 5*

Padmasambhava, Chokgyur Lingpa, Jamyang Khyentse Wangpo, Tulku
Urgyen Rinpoche, Orgyen Tobgyal Rinpoche, & others
Dispeller of Obstacles • *The Tara Compendium* •
Powerful Transformation • *Dakini Activity*

Yeshe Tsogyal: *The Lotus-Born*

Dakpo Tashi Namgyal: *Clarifying the Natural State*

Tsele Natsok Rangdröl: *Mirror of Mindfulness* • *Heart Lamp*

Chokgyur Lingpa: *Ocean of Amrita* • *The Great Gate* • *Skillful Grace* •
Great Accomplishment • *Guru Heart Practices*

Traktung Dudjom Lingpa: *A Clear Mirror*

Jamgön Mipham Rinpoche: *Gateway to Knowledge,
Vol. 1, Vol. 2, Vol. 3, & Vol. 4*

Tulku Urgyen Rinpoche: *Blazing Splendor* •
Rainbow Painting • *As It Is, Vol. 1 & Vol. 2* • *Vajra Speech* • *Repeating the
Words of the Buddha* • *Dzogchen Deity Practice* • *Vajra Heart Revisited*

Adeu Rinpoche: *Freedom in Bondage*

Khenchen Thrangu Rinpoche: *Crystal Clear*

Chökyi Nyima Rinpoche: *Bardo Guidebook* •
Collected Works of Chökyi Nyima Rinpoche, Vol. 1 & Vol. 2

Tulku Thondup: *Enlightened Living*

Orgyen Tobgyal Rinpoche: *Life & Teachings of Chokgyur Lingpa* •
Straight Talk • *Sublime Lady of Immortality*

Dzigar Kongtrül Rinpoche: *Uncommon Happiness*

Tsoknyi Rinpoche: *Fearless Simplicity* • *Carefree Dignity*

Marcia Binder Schmidt: *Dzogchen Primer* • *Dzogchen Essentials* • *Quintessential
Dzogchen* • *Confessions of a Gypsy Yogini* • *Precious Songs of Awakening
Compilation*

Erik Pema Kunsang: *Wellsprings of the Great Perfection* •
A Tibetan Buddhist Companion • *The Rangjung Yeshe Tibetan-English
Dictionary of Buddhist Culture & Perfect Clarity*

Uncommon Happiness

THE PATH OF THE
COMPASSIONATE WARRIOR

Dzigar Kongtrül Rinpoche

Compiled and Edited by
Marcia Binder Schmidt

Rangjung Yeshe Publications
Boudhanath, Hong Kong & Esby
2009

RANGJUNG YESHE PUBLICATIONS

www.rangjung.com
www.lotustreasure.com

Rangjung Yeshe Publications
526 Entrada Dr. Apt. 201
Novato, CA 94949 USA

First edition 2009

Printed in the
United States of America
1 2 3 4 5 6 7 8 9 13 12 11 10 09

Publication Data:

*Uncommon Happiness: The Path of the Compassionate
Warrior / Dzigar Kongtrül;* Edited & Compiled by
Marcia Binder Schmidt.

ISBN 978-962-7341-63-5 (pbk)
1. Religious Life—Buddhism 2. Buddhism—Doctrines
3. Vajrayana — Tibet. I. Title.

Cover Art by Dzigar Kongtrül [Jigmey Namgyal],
Cover. Design: Maryann Lipaj

Contents

Editor's Preface

DZIGAR KONGTRÜL RINPOCHE's teachings are permeated with an incredible compassion that is challenging to capture in the written word. His inspiring approach is laden with a *bodhichitta* that radiates great concern for us all. Working with this material has had a profound effect on even my hardened Dharma heart.

In the course of putting together this book, I experienced some interesting events that I boldly interpret as Rinpoche's blessings in validating the truth of the Dharma. I live part of the year in the Kathmandu Valley, in the mountain hermitage of Tulku Urgyen Rinpoche called Nagi Gompa. It is actually a nunnery. Our community encompasses many different types of people besides the nuns themselves, who are of varying backgrounds. For instance, there is a monk, the son of a deceased Nagi nun, who is seriously mentally ill. Quite kindly, the nunnery organization gave him a room at the lower monastery that houses the monks connected to Nagi.

Yearly, I do retreat at Nagi and sit several sessions in the outdoors away from my hut. I am particularly fond of practicing near a certain small cave. Every year at Nagi there is a great activity practice, a *drubchen* that goes on for nine days. One day, as I approached the cave, I saw the monk, Tsultrim, stringing electrical wiring to the cave. He assured me it was merely for a light, and that he would be sleeping in the cave only for the duration of the *drubchen*.

Of course, he didn't leave after the *drubchen* was over. Not only that, he stayed there all day blaring his radio, which he would turn down only when scolded. I went to other outside spots to practice, as the cave was not suitable with Tsultrim there. One day when I was close by, the noise from the radio became intolerable. I actively rushed over to confront him. As I marched towards the cave, crushing leaves and branches under my feet, I remembered Dzigar Kongtrül Rinpoche's teaching and tried to maintain a modicum of presence of mind as well as an attitude aimed at benefiting the monk. It was stupid to be angry, as I already knew that he was not mentally well and that arguing with a crazy person was hardly realistic. Keeping these thoughts in mind, I went up to the entrance of the cave. There was Tsultrim watching a soccer match on TV.

The incongruousness of the situation shifted my perspective entirely. I could only apologize for being such an unstable practitioner who was so easily distracted. It would be wonderful, I said if he could please try to understand that and be a support for my mindfulness. He reacted with immediate kindness and sympathy, never blared the radio or TV again, and left within a few days. That was an immediate sign to me that when applied, *bodhichitta* works. No matter how often I had heard these teachings and tried to practice them, it was only through the words of Dzigar Kongtrül Rinpoche that I had the determination to actually apply them.

The next interesting experience is connected to another mentally unstable resident of Nagi Gompa, this time a nun. Old Maya had been diagnosed as manic-depressive and was on medication.

Over the twenty-four years I lived next door to her, I witnessed several times when she went off her medication and experienced quite outrageous episodes resulting in hospitalization. She had a really good heart and was kind and funny, but didn't seem to be able to do any Dharma practice. When she died, the lamas thought that they should dispose of her body as quickly as possible and arranged for the cremation to be within twelve hours of her passing. However, it didn't happen that way, because she sat in *samadhi* for the entire next day, a state called *tukdam* in Tibetan. The signs of *tukdam* are that the heart remains warm, rigor mortis does not set in, and the body does not begin to deteriorate. The whole atmosphere around a practitioner who stays in *tukdam,* meditative composure, is serene and inspiring, which is exactly what it was like in our neighborhood. The power of Maya's good heart overrode all the difficult circumstances of her mental illness and medication. What a supreme validation of *bodhichitta!*

When reviewing these wonderful teachings, I felt that the way in which Rinpoche presented his commentary of Shantideva's *The Way of the Bodhisattva* stood on its own and deserved to be highlighted as an independent work. This incredible material was collected over three consecutive summers of teachings on this text that Rinpoche gave at Rangjung Yeshe Gomde in California from 2005 to 2007. In organizing them I mirrored the structure and arrangement of Patrul Rinpoche's *The Words of My Perfect Teacher,* second chapter on bodhichitta.

Dzigar Kongtrül Rinpoche's premise is extremely suitable to our times. To sum up this book, we suffer and are unhappy because we do not practice *bodhichitta.* It is simply a matter of intelligence to follow the well-validated results of the Buddha's research. These include self-reflection, changing one's focus from self to other, training in the four immeasurables, and arousing *bodhichitta* and engaging in it through the practice of the six *paramitas*. Dharma practice, Rinpoche reminds us over and over again in these teachings, needs to be more than mere theory. Dharma needs to be trained in, integrated into our lives, and embraced by wisdom.

I only hope that the wisdom imparted to us through Rinpoche's words as captured on these pages will inspire ready students and the goodness in publishing this book will extend the life of this precious master for the benefit of countless sentient beings.

Marcia Binder Schmidt

Uncommon Happiness

A True Caregiver

THE VARIOUS STUDIES AND PRACTICES of the Dharma are all essentially diverse ways of learning how to work with our mind. Let's say our mind is like a house. Before you decorate the house it needs to be cleaned, otherwise you will only be enhancing a mess. In a clean house, the true beauty of the decorations can really shine. Just as in this example, there is always a need to work with purifying our mind. To decorate our mind is through further study and practice of the Dharma.

What do we actually cleanse? Basically we cleanse our ignorant mind of whatever has sprung forth from that ignorance. The mind of ordinary sentient beings has a distinct sense of self. This sense of self is in a constant state of struggle, operating through the habits generated from ignorance. These patterns need to be studied and understood. This sense of clinging to the self has to be managed and transformed into something totally different. Without studying the habits and patterns of ordinary mind, we will be unable to transform the clinging to the self and to penetrate to the level of ignorant mind. From time to time we may temporarily be able to penetrate ignorance by the blessings of a very great master and our own devotion. But inevitably the habit comes back. All the struggles return, making it hard to fully rely upon ourselves and to genuinely develop our confidence.

There are as many varieties of habits as there are people existing in the world. In essence, however, there are the habitual patterns of the five different disturbing self-centered emotions: being attached, angry, proud, jealous, and unaware or stupid. One particular individual might have more difficulty or pain with anger rather than being jealous or prideful or attached. Another person might have serious problems with attachment, but not necessarily be aggressive, prideful, or jealous. These habits can be both gross and subtle. The study and practice of the Dharma is to really understand one's own habits, to have insight into them from a very clear, objective point of view, and then to find the skillful means to work with these habits.

The Dharma presents us with options. The deep wisdom of Dharma shows us how to find freedom and liberation from our own disturbing, painful habits. Without the Dharma, we would have to resort to our own limited understanding. We would be like flies trying futilely to get through a closed window. Not realizing that the transparency is actually solid glass, a fly will smash against the windowpane over and over again, eventually dropping dead. Without the wisdom and skillful means of the Dharma, we can end up feeling like that helplessly buzzing fly.

With the help of the Buddha, who is the teacher, the Dharma, which is the path, and the *Sangha*, our companions on this path, from deep within we strive to be free from our negative habits. We can no longer stand our confusion. The root cause of our suffering is our unmanaged, untamed mind, which cherishes the self. That is the problem.

Now we have arrived at the place where we do not want to let mind be chaotic and confused. We no longer want to be under the control of a self that randomly picks and senselessly chooses how to operate. Instead, we want to replace the sense of self and the habits developed out of ignorance with a true caregiver. We want to exchange our present mind's confusion and lack of sanity for the true caregiver of the mind that has the potential to embody wisdom. The wisdom inherent within us can discern what is favorable and what is not. We do not have to be controlled by instincts, but can question the very instincts that have gotten us into trouble. The instincts and urges that we feel so strongly inside result from the powerful momentum that has been created by habits. Without some self-reflection or questioning of our mind in this state, mind is very vulnerable and loses all its power of discernment.

As practitioners, we need to question and study our habits. We need to intimately examine the method of functioning that has caused us so much pain and suffering. Up until this point we have been completely under the power of confusion and disturbing emotions. These have guided our destinies. We have endured this pain in samsara for endless lifetimes. This is the truth, however painful and unbearable it may be. Now, finally, we have reached the place where we can do something about it. We must find within ourselves, in the core of our heart, renunciation. We need a certain confidence that we can actually abandon negative habitual patterns. We have the potential not only to renounce what is going on in our mind, but also to *replace* it with the enlightened mind. We need to have the confidence that enlightened mind is reachable. It is not something imported or stolen from outside, a foreign thing. Enlightened mind is present in this very confusion—inherent in this mind that at this very moment is ruled by habits, governed by ego, and filled with disturbing thoughts and emotions.

How can we find confidence in our present mind that is in such a deluded state? How do we bring this confidence out more and more and make it stronger? We need to rely on the Buddha, the teacher, the Dharma, his teachings, and the *Sangha,* our companions on the path. We need to connect with the three wisdoms: the hearing wisdom, the contemplative wisdom, and the meditative wisdom. With the help of these three wisdoms, our innate capacity can be brought out to the fullest extent.

Right now we have extremely favorable circumstances. Not only are we interested in the Dharma, but also we can meet teachers, hear and study teachings, and receive a spiritual teacher's guidance.

With the support of the perfect teacher and the teaching, when we study our mind, our pain, our habits, our self-cherishing and clinging, we can very clearly and intimately identify how pain and suffering are linked to the habits, how the habits are all linked to the disturbing emotions, the disturbing emotions are all linked to the cherishing and protecting of the self, the cherishing and protecting of the self is linked to the sense of clinging to a self, and finally the sense of clinging to a self is a product of confusion and ignorance. We can see this very clearly in our own experience. We have the potential to discern what is favorable and what is not, what supports our happiness and what opposes it. Based on this self-reflection we can gain the courage, the confidence, to overcome all our negative ignorant traits through the wisdom of the Dharma.

Self-reflection is not an end in itself. Rather, it is the key that opens the door to your innermost qualities, to buddha nature. It shows you the strength and confidence you already possess as a result of those innate qualities. This strength and confidence allows you to carry on with a sense of richness, of inner wealth.

Happiness and discernment can blossom from there. Once this discernment blossoms, it's not so difficult to get rid of or abandon the negative tendencies. It's as if you have a piece of metal that looks like gold and you treat it like gold, thinking it is very precious and will get you out of your impoverished state. You put it under your pillow to keep it safe and from time to time take it out to look at it. Then all of a sudden you find out that it's not gold—it's actually a piece of radioactive ore. Your whole relationship with it changes immediately. Once you know what it actually is and how dangerous it is, you will not struggle to get rid of it. Rather, you will try to get it out of your life as quickly as possible.

Similarly, it takes getting to that point to really know our own mind. We have to really know our own suffering, our disturbing emotions, and our struggle with our sense of self-importance. Truly know how these lead to so much more confusion and chaos in the form of actions that further perpetuate habits. When this kind of realization springs forth, we feel inspired to change our whole mind-set to something much more enlightened, to a completely different type of mind.

Again, in getting rid of all the layers of neurosis, we become very appreciative of the Dharma. We understand how it helps us to cleanse our mind and to replace what we have cleansed with sublime tools. If we do not replace the space we've cleansed with anything, it feels empty. It's quite nice to get rid of all the things that are crowding our room; however, we do need some furniture to make ourselves comfortable. People are afraid of emptiness because they think that if we get rid of everything, there will only be the empty. The Dharma suggests what to bring in after we have cleansed our mind, and it opens us to nurture and appreciate that.

Unconscious ignorant mind operates by cherishing and protecting the self. From this develops the mess of disturbing emotions, the habits they provide, and all the subsequent pain. But the clear, conscious mind that is steeped in the wisdom of the Buddhas, instead of protecting and cherishing the self, has expanded to include cherishing and protecting all others. At our current stage, to literally cherish all others and protect them is perhaps beyond our capacity, but the intention or wish to do so is certainly within our reach. To have that intention very alive inside of us as a deep yearning strengthens our determination to make progress every day, regardless of how much we are at odds with our old habits. This heartfelt intention sustains the practitioner's mind in loving-kindness and compassion and all the positive actions that spring forth from there.

It's not that we have no struggle here. We have a tremendous struggle against our habits. But we welcome that struggle, rather than thinking, "Oh, it should be a free ride to enlightenment." There is not going to be a free ride to enlightenment, a ride without any challenge. If that were possible, why wouldn't everyone be enlightened as easily as they intended? Such a vision is not realistic, nor is it exciting. We have to see ourselves rising from our own cocoon, rising from our own old ignorant mind.

Samsara and nirvana exist within you. Samsara is made of our mind, as is nirvana. Without samsara, there is not going to be nirvana. Without a dweller in samsara, there is not going to be an achiever of nirvana. Of course, according to absolute truth there are no notions of nirvana or samsara. However, within the relative way of viewing reality, because we intend to attain nirvana, there must be samsara to overcome.

In this kind of thinking, every possibility is a great thrill. Let's say, generally speaking, that we don't enjoy someone's aggression coming towards us. We tend to dread this aggression, especially if it's from people dwelling under the same roof. Spouses dread each other's wrath or temper. Children dread upsetting their parents and unleashing their anger. Aggression disturbs our peace, and that disturbance causes us dread and fear. With a bit of study, we can understand that it is not the aggression that destroys our peace. It is our mind's weakness in patience that destroys our peace and creates that fear. If you know for a fact that someone is not going to harm you, you have no fear. No matter how much other beings are intending to harm you, even if they swarm around you like a cloud of small flies in summertime, you don't have fear, because you feel secure. The experience of threat is due to our own lack of security, our own lack of stability, our own lack of unshakable strength and patience, and this makes us feel overwhelmed by aggression, big or small.

Bodhisattvas develop unshakable patience. No matter how many flies are swarming around threatening to get a good bite of your skin, if you have attained stability in the training, you cannot be harmed. In reality it's exciting to have difficult circumstances and problems like aggression come into your life so that you can actually work with them. Without some practice, you are never going to get there. Knowing that, all of these challenges are welcomed.

Bodhisattvas take joy in encountering challenges. They are not interested in some kind of vague hypothetical challenge, but in real-life situations—not only challenges but disasters as well, because from the perspective of practice these situations provide great opportunities. The question then becomes, "Is this a challenge? Is this really a disaster, or is this a great gift?" What seems to be a disaster or a challenge is a gift to bodhisattvas, and they welcome it.

In this way, samsara becomes a delightful place to live, especially for the bodhisattvas who are training their minds to become free from the deep-rooted weaknesses in the duality of ego. Everything becomes good, and this is a view that we as practitioners, as amateur bodhisattvas, are trying to learn. Right now we are amateurs, but someday we will become the real thing, and this is one's own choice. The key to it is to sit with one's mind, to study one's mind, to learn one's mind, to find the transcripts of one's mind in the books and in the teachings. Transcripts shed light on the mind. Use the teaching as a transcript, and then understand that the real teachings are in one's mind. The books illuminate what takes place in the mind. When we approach the teaching in this manner, the teachings are not separate from our mind. The teachings *are* our mind.

In light of what we need to cleanse and what we need to nurture within our minds, the teachings become a great source of relief. As I said earlier, if we don't have the teachings, we must resort to our own intelligence, our own wisdom; and if we do not have something greater than our limited intelligence and wisdom in the midst of all the confusion, habits, and conflicting emotions that overwhelm us, we become worse than the fly that is trying fruitlessly to escape, hitting his head against the windowpane. We may even become fanatical in our desperation. The fly, after all, is just trying to get out. Maybe he is hitting his head a little too hard, but he is not harming anyone—he is simply exhausting himself. When we human beings become fanatical out of our own desperation, we harm not only ourselves, but others as well. Driven by the immense power of confusion and disturbing emotions, we act in ways that further disturb us and jeopardize our well-being, not only in this lifetime, but also in many lifetimes to come.

Teachings are a respite because they provide us a pathway to understand ourselves, a pathway to relieve ourselves from the burdens, habits, and confusion created by disturbing emotions and ignorant mind. The Dharma truly does point us to who we really are, what we are really capable of, and what we really can do with our lives and our minds. Generally speaking, an ordinary sentient being can only become an ordinary sentient being. The teachings describe how an ordinary sentient being can become a Buddha.

This is not just a description of how it could be for you and how it would be so wonderful if you could get there. If teachings only described a state that could be so wonderful, but didn't show you the path to get there, you would feel like a hungry dog looking up at a chicken hanging just out of reach. You have no way to get up there. But the teachings are not like that.

They guide us step-by-step as to how we can actually emerge out of our cocoon of ignorance, out of our disturbing emotions and self-centeredness. What are the transformations to be made? How are those transformations possible, and how are those transitions made in reality? The teachings show this all to us very clearly, and therefore we feel very appreciative of them. That is why the Buddha is the refuge for us: He embodies the enlightened qualities that are within the reach of every one of us.

Transformation

IF WE'RE DEEPLY ADDICTED to a substance, then the triumph of overcoming substance abuse is a great release. Likewise, to gain some independence from the raging conflicting emotions that consume us much of the time in subtle ways has a powerful after-effect. That freedom encourages us to replace the conflicted mind and habitual tendencies with something much better—an abundance of loving-kindness and compassion. We will see how loving-kindness and compassion can enrich our minds. When the negative tendencies are removed and transformed, we are able to generate all the positive qualities that are inherent to mind.

Our tendency to cherish the self, protect the self, and be exclusively focused on the self can be changed with a simple and effective method. We remove our self as the focus of cherishing and protection, and replace the self with others. When we do this, we're not getting rid of cherishing. We're not getting rid of protecting—just changing the focus from our self and putting others first. The new cherishing is developed through logic and reasoning. To put ourselves as the focus of cherishing and protecting has no logic. It is just instinct and habit. And it is never the case that it brings us more happiness. I'll paraphrase from *The Way of the Bodhisattva:* "If taking yourself as the focus of cherishing and protecting achieved happiness, you would already be happy, because this has been going on for a long time. In truth, however, this has not worked; therefore, we are all in samsara." The *tathagatas* have not taken the self as the focus of cherishing and protecting, but rather have taken others as the focus. They have achieved *buddhahood*, which is proof that it does work.

This can be reasoned from cause and from effect. Just as we desire happiness, so does everyone else. Just as we desire freedom from suffering, so does everyone else—so why discriminate? The logic here is to make *everyone* who desires happiness important, *everyone* who desires freedom from suffering important, and therefore put everyone in the center of our cherishing and protecting, making everyone's well-being and freedom our focus. That is from the cause side. From the effect side, when we put the focus of cherishing and protecting on the self, what surges out are the disturbing emotions. But if we make others, all sentient beings, the primary focus, loving-kindness and compassion surge forth.

From every angle we can see that it makes sense to do this. The only problem standing in our way is the habitual pattern of doing otherwise. Working with that pattern will take some time and struggle. These tendencies of cherishing and protecting are difficult to get rid of. But changing our focus can make an enormous difference. Since we are already very familiar with cherishing and protecting, simply changing the focus of these behaviors can have an incredibly good result. Knowing what we have to work with makes a lot of sense. Whether we are driving East or West, driving is driving. We are already familiar with driving, so why not see if we can change directions?

We all know the sorts of concerns that come out of cherishing, loving, and caring. Every aspect of these emotions is very familiar. Up until this point, it's all been in relation to the self; that's what's messed it up. Now the focus is on directing the same feelings, the same emotions, not onto the self, but outward. The Mahayana teachings in the Buddhist canon are incredibly wise, intelligent, and deep in wisdom. In the Hinayana the emphasis is more on what to get rid of, what to eliminate. In the Mahayana it is on transformation, changing our attitude or focus. For someone who has actually never loved, to imagine loving others is very difficult. For someone who has never felt compassion, to imagine feeling an abundance of compassion is nearly impossible. But someone who has felt a tremendous amount of love and compassion for himself is capable of extending that to others.

The only challenge, really, is habit. Habit tugs away at us to follow in the same old rut. Still, remedying this is easier than trying to generate something we find inconceivable. We progress on the path of loving others as we love ourselves, caring for others as we care for ourselves, being compassionate to others as we are compassionate to ourselves, being concerned for others as we are concerned for ourselves. Progress comes in finding the freedom to do so clearly and cleanly, without confusion or reservations. In this way, freedom becomes abundant in our life. Joy and contentment become abundant in our life. This process takes some time, because the heart needs to catch up with the head. But retraining the heart to respond to what the head commands it to do can be successful, sooner or later.

There is an incredible intelligence at work here, in which the thinking and reasoning are very clear. The heart has to follow the head. Heart is the experiencer of pain and pleasure. The heart tastes life, so when it feels all of this freedom and joy, a sense of great relief and contentment arises. When compassion's positive qualities touch the heart that generates the compassion, the heart is sustained in happiness by the very thing it has created. The heart needs the thinking mind to lead it on the path, but truly the feelings spontaneously follow.

So my point here is that to train one's mind and heart at the same time is the Buddhist path, the Mahayana path. The basic makeup of mind is not changed or eliminated. Instead, we use the innate tendencies to create a different effect, by training in a different focus. There is an interesting statement in a Sutra text that says, "Where do the *tathagatas* come from? *Tathagatas* are given birth to by egos." Generally speaking, egos are what prevent us from becoming *tathagatas*. We get rid of the focus of the self by placing others where one's self previously was and then learning how to generate loving-kindness, compassion, goodness, and protection for others. This method of transformation makes the teachings truly accessible and comprehensible.

Hopefully we can learn all of this in more depth as we go into Shantideva's teachings, and hopefully we can also discuss how it makes sense to do this based on our own experiences. We can study the ways this was done in the past and also discuss how we can actually integrate this with our own experience. Imagine the effect this would have on our mind. When we access the need, it makes us very strongly interested—unless from time to time we just fall asleep. Sometimes, we all want to ignore what's good for us. We know that eating salad is good, but sometimes we just don't want to eat salad! We avoid the salad and eat junk food instead. Of course, this happens sometimes. I encourage students to really examine what is taught here. See how it can be integrated with your own personal experience, and consider its effects, and the need for this kind of practice. When you examine them in this way, the teachings will have a lot of meaning. Moreover, the teachings will become an integral part of your life. When this does not take place and the teachings are not able to become an essential part of your life, something else will fill that spot: Work becomes essential; survival in this modern world becomes the essential meaning of life. Hustling and bustling become essential. The survival instinct that we secure in these ways becomes the most essential aspect of our life. In doing so, however, the world fails to actually secure its happiness.

If someone is to become a practitioner, a true student of Dharma, that person has to know that practice is an essential part of one's life, intimately interwoven with one's own experience. Of course, we need to keep our jobs. We need to be responsible with our family. We need to do a lot of different things in our lives, but none of these become essential. Rather, they become important in support of what we find the most meaningful in life—becoming a student of Dharma, a practitioner of Dharma. All these other things are just simply in support of that. In this way, then, our interest in the Dharma and practice will not wane over time. It gets stronger as we directly experience its results and benefits.

Otherwise, life's demands and stresses to keep things in relative order—even just paying the bills so that we can have a decent life—can sweep us away so that we ignore our Dharma practice and studies. We never even think that we are missing much of an opportunity. That's because we haven't yet truly realized how beneficial Dharma is for our mind. Ultimately, the Dharma has the capacity to free us from suffering. Suffering is something that may be tolerable in the short term, but the prospect of suffering over many, countless lifetimes is not.

You need to study the Dharma to have some kind of revolution in your mind, and to understand how this revolution is relevant to life's essential meaning—not just to survival and covering the basics, even though you also need to take care of that. This kind of dedication gives you a sense of strong determination to make your interest in the Dharma path come to fruition through your own efforts, year after year after year. Once you reach that point, the teacher's job is done.

Until then, however, the teacher has a certain amount of responsibility to oversee students so that they do not become "high school dropouts." Parents have responsibility to see their children through high school; after that, they're on their own. Similarly, students need to get to the point of seeing how the Dharma changes their mind for the better. Hopefully, my teaching here in accordance with *The Way of the Bodhisattva* will bring you closer to understanding the Dharma from your own experience and to seeing how it is an integral part of the meaning of life in a very positive way. I don't know if we will get completely to that point, but hopefully we can draw closer to it.

This is an orientation to the teachings in general. It is also an introduction to the bodhisattva's path, the practice of truly changing our mind and what that can mean for our well-being and freedom from suffering. In the following sessions, I hope to elucidate mind, both certain particular problems of mind and also how those problems can actually become an asset simply by changing our focus. I will try to show how some of those tendencies are in one way a problem, and on the other hand can actually be a conduit that carries us to being a bodhisattva and the practitioner we want to become. I will explore how the teachings can become a resource for our intelligence and wisdom, and a transcript of our mind. I will use quotes and take guidance from the text of *The Way of the Bodhisattva*, in which a great bodhisattva, the Indian *mahapandita* Shantideva, elucidates the path on which to travel. In this process, we will journey from a confused mind to a clear mind. The text is a support to effect the true transformation of mind, the transformation of our self-centered mind to a *bodhi* heart.

Mind is actually the teaching itself and needs to be understood through personal experience. These experiences will lead us to renunciation and heighten our interest, which makes us solid practitioners and sustains us on the path. I hope to weave all this together. These are the points I want to emphasize. Please do engage in questioning and discussions as fully as possible. Don't be shy. This is not the time to be shy. We have to learn, and whatever I have to offer I will offer.

The Path

BEFORE I GET INTO THE BODY of instructions on the bodhisattva trainings, I want to give an overview of the whole Buddhist path. The Buddhist teachings can be divided into two categories. In the first are the Buddha's own words spoken during his lifetime, as recorded in the sutras, called *kha* in Tibetan. Then there are the commentaries that were written by Buddha's disciples—arhats and the great *mahapanditas* of the noble land of India, such as Nagarjuna, Aryadeva, Asanga, and Vasubandhu. The texts they composed, elucidating the Buddha's teachings, are collectively known as *tencho* in Tibetan or *shastra* in Sanskrit. Whether it is the *kha*, Buddha's teachings in his own words, or the *tencho*, the words of his disciples, the great teachers of India, Tibet, or any other place, all Buddhist teachings fall into three categories: Vinaya, Sutra, and Abhidharma.

All teachings have two qualities. The first is that they protect the student by providing the intelligence, wisdom, and skillful means to prevent the individual from taking a rebirth in the lower realms. In other words, they help whoever studies them to reduce the afflictive emotions and their cause, the tendency towards clinging to the self, and the root cause of that, which is ignorance. If the teachings don't affect the mind in this way, then they will not protect beings from falling down into the lower realms. Teachings must have the quality of remedying confused mind. The second quality of the teachings is the capacity to bring the student to higher realms and a greater appreciation of his or her own nature, an understanding of and ability to rely on these exalted characteristics. So these are the two qualities of the teachings: protecting us from our disturbing emotions and how these can bring us down; and illuminating and thus helping us appreciate our own nature and its qualities.

The three categories of the teachings Vinaya, Sutra, and Abhidharma—form the path to realization. Essentially, to obtain enlightenment we need discipline, meditation, and wisdom. Without discipline and a change in our approach to life, we, as confused sentient beings, will always do the same thing and jeopardize our own freedom and happiness. Therefore, the Vinaya must be practiced. Vinaya is basically taking a vow, be it Hinayana, Mahayana, or Vajrayana. These vows protect us. These vows guard us against indulging in our habits. The vows are mindfulness practice. By following the precepts, we train our being in a new approach. We train ourselves to refrain from past negative habits, and then through the vow and precepts we practice to increase and discipline ourselves in positive actions.

The Vinaya teachings are the follow-up to teachings on karma. We try to distance ourselves from karma that is unfavorable to us. We need to have some discipline to do so. We try to engage in karma that is positive to our well-being and our future lives. We endeavor to learn how to engage more efficiently and precisely. We must practice the Vinaya to attain enlightenment. Whether it is in the Hinayana, Mahayana, or Vajrayana, everyone must practice the Vinaya, the teachings of discipline. Without discipline, there is no leap to enlightenment. That is why the teachings of the Buddha and his disciples all fall in one way into the Vinaya.

The second category is the Sutra teachings. These include instructions on meditation: how to cultivate skillful means in order to get a clear, deep insight into one's nature, as well as how to cultivate the enlightened qualities that our nature offers. We are taught to skillfully follow the tradition of the various methods discovered by the Buddha. The instructions open up many possibilities for a more efficient and greater meditation practice that removes ignorance and obscurations. Hence our nature can then outshine the obscurations and purify them. All of these teachings are called Sutra teachings. We can have very profound discipline, but without meditation the path to enlightenment is incomplete. The Sutra teachings are thus the second category of the teachings of the Buddha.

The final category is the Abhidharma. Abhidharma is made up of true statements of how things actually are, in both the absolute and relative sense. It consists of teachings on the wisdom aspect—discovering the wisdom within our mind. How things are in the absolute sense is *shunyata*, empty of any true existence. How things are in the relative sense is illusory. Samsara begins with the illusion; nirvana is the cessation of that illusion. The teachings explain how to realize illusion as illusion, and how to end illusion and come to fully experience the cessation of that, which is nirvana itself. Nirvana is constantly present and constantly unchanging. It's always present while the illusion is happening, in the same way that a white screen remains unchangingly present even as all the colors of the movie continue to play on its surface.

Discipline is very important, therefore, in the Vinaya teachings. Meditation is also very important, hence the Sutra teachings.

Wisdom is very important to enlightenment, thence the Abhidharma teachings. From this perspective, we see the three kinds
of training needed on the path to enlightenment: training in discipline, meditation, and wisdom.

There is yet another way of categorizing the Buddha's teachings, namely in terms of scriptural teachings and realization teachings. The scriptural teachings are found in books: They are the
teachings that are explained by the teacher, the teachings that you
read, hear, study, and contemplate. Essentially, these have more to
do with the relative aspect of truth. The teachings of realization
are on the essential awareness that actually brings the individual
to a state of nirvana. That is the recognition of *shunyata* itself,
egolessness, the realization of the absolute state. The absolute
state, nature, or truth is the nature of all phenomena. Nirvana
is always pure, never changing. It is the absence of confused
perception or delusion. Even though in the absolute nirvana is
unchanging, individual beings who are confused, caught up in
the relative mind of obscurations, do not benefit from absolute
truth or nirvana. However, the fundamental nature of absolute
truth or nirvana provides the possibility for the deluded individual to slowly and gradually wake up to the truth by purifying
obscurations and ignorance.

Prior to that point, the ground of enlightenment is in all
beings, but the path has not begun. When the process of awakening begins, one has entered the path. When an individual has
completely gone through the process of waking up to the absolute truth, that person literally possesses the nirvana that was
always there but was not actualized. When the obscurations are
no longer a hindrance to seeing the absolute nature, you repos-
sess what was innately present. Now you can fully engage with

nirvana. This is the ultimate destiny for all beings, because everyone is seeking nirvana.

Maitreya Buddha has said that all sentient beings possess the instinctive longing for freedom from pain, the instinctive longing for happiness. This instinctive longing for happiness, for freedom from pain and suffering, is the intuitive intelligence of the buddha nature present in all beings expressing itself. Otherwise, how could an instinct exist if it had no way to express itself? If there were no way to find ultimate happiness or freedom, why would that instinct exist in the first place? Right up until the point of complete nirvana that instinct is unfulfilled. No ultimate happiness is achieved, since one has not completely freed oneself from pain and the cause of pain.

The ultimate destiny of all beings is enlightenment. It is always present, but because we are confused and totally overwhelmed by delusion, the natural nirvana of the enlightened nature remains only a disposition. By disposition I mean a propensity to slowly and gradually work to fulfill a particular destiny. The disposition of an apple seed, for example, is to become an apple tree. The minds of all sentient beings have the disposition to become enlightened, and the intuitive, intelligent aspect of this is expressed by their longing for happiness and freedom from suffering—but just that alone is not going to do it.

We need more clarity, understanding, and realization of the truth, the wisdom aspect. Then we need meditation to purify the obscurations and habits. We also need the Vinaya, the discipline to do this. The essence of the Dharma is the realization of suchness, of the natural nirvana. This is free of concepts. It is the experience of the truth. Concepts point us in the right direction, but concepts themselves are dualistic, and thus are blind to the actual truth itself. When we don't completely shed all our concepts and instead engage in them, we are in relative mind, not absolute mind.

Realization of the absolute truth that resides in the minds of the buddhas, bodhisattvas, and great masters is always free of concepts. In this state there is no arising, dwelling, or ceasing. Concepts, however, have arising, dwelling, and ceasing. The scriptural Dharma is conceptual, but we need it in order to get to the ultimate realization. The scriptural Dharma, its study and contemplation, is like a bridge. Once you've crossed the bridge, you no longer need it, because you've gotten to where you wanted to go. However, even when you don't need the bridge for yourself, it can be important for others. Similarly, scriptural Dharma is very important in communicating with others.

Now, a bodhisattva is an individual who has come onto the path to enlightenment, and has achieved partial purification and partial obtainment of the enlightened qualities. Entering the path of the bodhisattva is the beginning of the ripening of the seed of enlightened mind. Until that happens, there is not even the ability to hear this truth. Even if you happen to hear about it, you won't believe it, because you are simply not interested. When there is interest in not only hearing of it but in deeply believing it, this is the time of awakening. From the time of the seed's awakening all the way up until full enlightenment is the bodhisattva path. In the path of the bodhisattva, there are five paths and ten *bhumis*. The five paths are the path of accumulation, the path of engagement, the path of seeing, the path of meditation, and the path of no more learning.

The path of accumulation is when one actually, seriously, and deeply turns away from ignorance and the cause of suffering and generates the aspiration to be enlightened. This enlightenment is not sought after for oneself, but for the benefit of all sentient beings, so that they themselves may attain freedom from suffering and enlightenment. When such an aspiration for enlightenment is given birth to and is then supported by one or many positive actions, this is the outset of the path of accumulation. On the path of accumulation the seed of awakening is planted, through the hearing, contemplating, and meditating wisdoms. Through these three aspects one gains more insight. The power of these is called merit, which will bring one to real experience.

On the path of engagement, one actually learns about the absolute truth and has an understanding of the view of emptiness through meditation. This understanding or experience of the ultimate truth of *shunyata* is not completely naked or clear. It is more of an intellectual understanding than a true experience of *shunyata* or egolessness. But the way to the direct experience of *shunyata* is via the path of engagement. The path of engagement involves a sense of making *shunyata* your life.

On the path of seeing, the way has started to become your life. During this path, there is the beginning of maturation, which unfolds in the path of meditation. The path of meditation is the maturation of directly realizing *shunyata*. One experiences all phenomena as illusory, as a means to perfect one's enlightened activities to benefit beings.

There are two kinds of obscurations that need to be purified on the path to enlightenment: the emotional obscurations and the cognitive obscurations. Emotional obscurations are the five disturbing emotions of passion, aggression, stupidity, jealousy, and arrogance and all their various aspects. The reason they are called emotional obscurations is because our emotions are involved, and also because they come from a sense of clinging to a self. How are they obscurations? When we are engaged in, say, anger, we lose clarity; caught up in the experience of anger, our clarity is blocked. We lose not only the experience of truth, but of any opportunity to realize the truth.

The cognitive obscurations are basically dualistic mind—mind that actually believes things to be real, that believes subjective mind to be real, the objective world to be real, mind that believes there is some kind of intrinsic nature or existence to everything. The cognitively obscured mind does not see all things as illusory or dreamlike. It sincerely believes that this table is real, this book is real, this statue is real, this cup is real, this hand is real—that every aspect of one's feelings and perceptions is real. Believing something to be real is the fundamental cognitive obscuration, which prevents one from seeing the illusory nature of things, their ultimate emptiness.

The emotional obscurations are purified on the path of seeing. Then it takes ten *bhumis* to purify the cognitive obscurations. The view of the absolute truth of *shunyata* or egolessness that one sees on the path of seeing is increased on the path of meditation. There is nothing new on the path of meditation in terms of seeing, but one's perspective or experience of it is increased and strengthened, like a waxing moon that over time increases its light and clarifies the darkness.

Likewise, what you experience on the path of seeing is the absolute truth of egolessness, the experience of which increases over time and thus purifies the obscurations. When all the obscurations, both emotional and cognitive, are purified, you have attained Buddhahood. At this point you have accomplished the final path, the path of no more learning. You know the absolute truth as well as the entire variety of things there are to know. You have two wisdoms: the wisdom of knowing the absolute truth, the suchness aspect, and the wisdom of knowing everything there is to know.

To sum up, the bodhisattva path consists of five paths and ten *bhumis*.[1] In all of these five paths and ten *bhumis,* the main thing the bodhisattva actually practices is *bodhichitta.*

Training

START WITH THE PRACTICE of the four immeasurables every day. When you meditate on the four immeasurables of equanimity, loving-kindness, compassion, and sympathetic joy, something sort of sets off an alarm inside of you. This practice lightens up your tendencies to hold a grudge, to be partial, or to be excessively attached.

There is a story from a Tibetan comedian that illustrates the tendency to recite prayers without truly embodying them in our actions. This comedian was in a village where the dogs barked all the time. One particular dog was really mean to him, coming into his room and terrorizing him. Anyway, one day the man made a trap for the dog, so that next time the dog entered the room a big stone would drop on its head. Later that day, the man was doing his evening prayers, saying, "May all sentient beings have happiness and the causes of happiness." Usually this went quite smoothly, but that particular day it was a bit rough. Something was bothering him. He thought, "Well, maybe I shouldn't do quite this much." He went back and replaced the big stone with a piece of wood. When he finished his evening prayers and said, "May all sentient beings have happiness and the causes of happiness," it went quite smoothly. The next morning he got up early and stumbled out the door, triggering the trap. The piece of wood hit him on the head, and suddenly he realized that if he had left the rock there yesterday it would have killed, not the dog, but him. It was a wake up call to really pay attention to what we recite and take it to heart not as mere lip service but as something that we implement with our actions.

When you meditate on the four immeasurables and are giving birth to the aspiration *bodhichitta,* any of the neuroses that are there in opposition to that can flash like lights before us. This is the opportunity for you to really get into it and see. What was it that you did yesterday that was so partial? What was it that you did yesterday that was so unkind? What was it that you did yesterday that was so uncompassionate? How is this current state of mind? Are you holding a grudge, clinging to the self, or holding on to certain expectations? Once the red lights beep in your meditation, get into it, come to know it very clearly, understand, and then be cleansed by meditation practice. If you can actually cleanse your heart right on the spot with loving-kindness, compassion, sympathetic joy, or equanimity that is wonderful. If not, work towards cleansing. Sometimes it takes a while. Keep at it a little bit at a time.

Training in this a way, one day you will actually have the meditation of loving-kindness, compassion, sympathetic joy, and equanimity without any flashing red lights. Your deeds of yesterday and today will be totally imperturbable and influenced by those practices.

Also contemplate how to engage in the practice of generosity. When acting the opposite to generosity, immediately think, "I should be very generous." Study the problems of the mind that is not generous and get to know that pain more intimately. Slowly inspire yourself to be generous. Also, with the mind that is not disciplined in virtuous acts, instead of expecting to be disciplined all of a sudden, ask what is that mind that is not disciplined like? Examine your mind that is steeped in being carried away by its own energy and that of negative habits. Study them, understand them, and then slowly get to know the pain of unwholesome mind more intimately so that one can actually develop renunciation towards that. Inspire yourself to get rid of these habits and then slowly discipline yourself in the virtuous mind.

Generally in the training of the four immeasurables, one actually trains in the equanimity practice first and then one trains in the loving-kindness, compassion, and sympathetic joy, sequentially. Most of you know the book by Patrul Rinpoche, *The Words of My Perfect Teacher*. It contains clear instructions on how to engage in these four immeasurables, equanimity, love, compassion, and sympathetic joy. Once one is quite trained in the four immeasurables, give birth to aspiration *bodhichitta,* a genuine wish to attain enlightenment for the sake of all mother sentient beings, free them from suffering, and establish them in enlightenment as well.

You can train progressively, first seeing yourself and others as equal and then exchanging yourself with others. Finally, train in cherishing others more than yourself. These are all specific trainings that you can do according to your lineage's traditions to make changes in your mind. It takes a little while of training before your heart will catch up with your head. As the heart becomes slowly purified, cleansed by the power and blessings of what you are thinking, eventually it can actually make a leap to join in with the head. It is very helpful to be patient. Try to understand the reasoning and logic much more clearly, and slowly let your heart follow the reasoning and intention.

However, when we do the practice of the four immeasurables and give birth to *bodhichitta* right now, we are immature bodhisattvas so there is going to be some inconsistency with how we feel loving-kindness, compassion, sympathetic joy, and equanimity. It's not going to be completely stable, but the effort counts the most. Putting effort into practicing the four immeasurables every day in our life and giving rise to aspiration *bodhichitta* really does seem to work as a protection against our own old habits, the disturbing emotions that surge uncontrollably and take up space in our mind. It also works as a way to cleanse them when they do arise and also to transform them. To practice the four immeasurables every day is highly recommended. Begin by simply reading it aloud: "May all sentient beings have happiness and the causes of happiness," and so on. Then spend some time contemplating the practice and trying to generate a sense of loving-kindness and compassion along with what you recite.

The whole point of becoming a student of the Buddha Dharma is to transform mind. If this does it, which I think it does very well, then we should cherish this. I would highly recommend you to do the practice of the four immeasurables before giving rise to the aspiration *bodhichitta* and before practicing seeing yourself and others as equal, exchanging yourself for others, and cherishing others more than yourself. Take the four immeasurables as a main practice, to follow every day. Spend maybe ten minutes on each of the four immeasurables, and then in the end give rise to aspiration *bodhichitta.* If you can do this, then all the teachings you have received on *bodhichitta* can merge into this practice and slowly come to shape it. To develop a foundation that supports your studies and practice is very valuable.

To simplify things, let's engage in a guided meditation on all four immeasurables:

Loving Kindness

LET'S BEGIN WITH loving-kindness. Close your eyes, and imagine limitless space. In the same way that space is limitless, sentient beings are innumerable. The deepest desire and longing of all sentient beings is for happiness and the causes of happiness.

Now, meditate on your own desire and longing for happiness and on the causes and conditions of happiness. This desire is constant. Just as this is the case for you, clearly realize that it is the same for all sentient beings. You and all others have the same longing, the same deep desire and wish. There is no difference between you and other sentient beings.

How intense this longing is, and how constant! There are so many ways in which we try to achieve this happiness. Realize that the same happens to all beings: There is no difference between you and other sentient beings.

Because we are caught in our own self-absorption, we fail to realize what is happening to all sentient beings. Try to eliminate this self-absorption. Try to understand what is universal to the minds of all sentient beings. Make a connection between what is happening in you and what is happening in everybody else. Recognize that all sentient beings are equal.

And then wish that all beings, including yourself, may be happy and obtain the causes and conditions of happiness, on both the relative and ultimate level.

In terms of the relative level, think of all the ways in which sentient beings wish to have their needs fulfilled, from the basic needs of a hungry person who wants food, to anything that could possibly be desired or wished for. Make the aspiration prayer for all these wishes to be fulfilled and for all the causes and conditions of happiness to arise.

And then pray, over and over again,

> May all sentient beings be happy and obtain the causes and conditions of happiness.

Using yourself as an example, you can come to know the wish of all beings, the universal wish. Aspire to fulfill the universal wish of all sentient beings. Why limit your prayer to yourself? Why limit it to only some people? Make your aspiration include all sentient beings.

Is there any point in wishing solely for your own happiness? Is there any point in wishing for only some people to be happy? Realize that this kind of segregation has never made any great difference in our lives or in the world, and is based upon our biased mind. This bias consists of your own attachments. Your attachments have not led you in a good direction in the past, and will not lead you in a good direction in the future.

Therefore, try to make your wish impartial. Cover the whole of space, and include all sentient beings. Then think,

> May all sentient beings be happy and obtain the causes and conditions of happiness.

Repeat this in your mind again and again. Go deeper and deeper into what you feel as you repeat this line of the prayer over and over.

Then look at how intensely your mind is dedicated to your own comfort and happiness. Recognize your mind's deep longing, your constant effort, your twenty-four-hours-a-day, nonstop desire. Realize that it is the same for all beings, and make their longing and desire equally important to your own.

Think of how wonderful it would be if every sentient being could attain happiness. Then think of yourself or a small number of beings attaining happiness and what a limited achievement that would be. Why not pray for *all* beings to attain happiness and the causes of happiness?

And then repeat,

> May all beings be happy; may all beings obtain the causes and conditions of happiness.

When you are happy, how does it touch you? When you obtain the causes and conditions of happiness, how do you feel? How do you experience joy and happiness? It is exactly the same for all sentient beings, so try to visualize this, repeating the prayer in your mind again and again and again.

From time to time, reflect on how hard your heart has become, in that it does not feel very much nor does it contain the genuine wish for the happiness of all sentient beings.

Develop a sense of sadness and renunciation about this, and again wish for all sentient beings to be happy and to enjoy the causes and conditions of happiness. Repeat the prayer over and over again.

And then think how wonderful it would be if you could open your heart wider, make it more tender, and deepen your concern and care for all beings. Pray for the welfare of all: Inspire yourself, make this wish, and then repeat the first line of the prayer to yourself again and again and again.

Realize that the attainment of every positive worldly and spiritual quality—the path to the higher realms of worldly nature, such as the human and god realms; the path of liberation from samsara; and the path of enlightenment—depends on our genuine wish to develop a good heart. Realize the significance of cultivating a good heart, and wish that all sentient beings may be happy and obtain the causes and conditions of happiness.

Think of all the goodness that you have received, both in the past and the present. This goodness is the result of the kindness of all sentient beings. Someone other than yourself has given it to you.

If it were not for others, you would not have a body to be born into. You would be wandering in the intermediate state like a lost soul, forever and ever. So this body, and the privilege of sight, hearing, and all the other senses and functions of the body, are received as a gift from others. Here, the significant others are your own parents. By remembering the various ways in which your parents expressed their kindness to you, make the wish to express the same kindness to all sentient beings, thinking,

> May all beings be happy and obtain the causes and conditions of happiness.

Next, consider how you would not have survived if you had been abandoned at birth. Instead, you were embraced and nurtured, fed, clothed, educated, and shown how to fit into society. As the capable adult you are now, your qualities have come from the kindness of others, particularly from the significant kindness expressed by your parents. On this basis, wish that all beings may be happy and attain the causes and conditions of happiness.

Realize that all beings have at some point been your parents. Just as your current parents have cared for you in this life, all other beings have cared for you in the past. Feel the deep kindness that you have received from your own parents, and remember that you have received the same kindness from all beings without exception. On this basis repeat,

> May all beings be happy and obtain the causes and conditions of happiness.

In all the various ways mentioned here, and in other ways as well, try to make this wish genuine. You know it is genuine when you feel that your constant longing for personal happiness and all the various ways in which you attempt to achieve that becomes a longing for the happiness of all sentient beings.

Be glad if this aspiration arises naturally. Until that point arrives, vow to train your mind so that one day you will reach it. Pray to the buddhas and bodhisattvas for the welfare of all beings and for your mind to reach that point.

Compassion

NOW WE COME to compassion. Think about all the physical, mental, and emotional suffering that you want to avoid, and all the unfortunate circumstances, causes, and conditions that threaten your well-being.

You want to be free from suffering and the causes and conditions of suffering. How reactive you are, and how immediately you move to reject, abandon, or distance yourself from your suffering! In various ways, successful or not, you try to overcome and eliminate the causes and conditions of suffering.

Your involvement in eliminating your suffering is constant and intense. You don't appreciate suffering. Realize that sentient beings are all the same, and that what's happening inside you happens inside everybody. This longing and these reactions are universal.

Then think about why you are only concerned with yourself. It is far more appropriate to be concerned about the suffering of all sentient beings. Therefore, wish for all beings to be free from suffering and the causes and conditions of suffering. How unnatural it is to be concerned solely with your own suffering when actually everybody is in the same situation!

Wish that all beings might be free from suffering and the causes and conditions of suffering. Repeat this wish in your mind, over and over again,

> May all beings be free from suffering and the causes and conditions of suffering.

Think of how intense suffering can be when it arises in your own mind, and recognize that the pain, suffering, anguish, and depression of all other sentient beings are equally unbearable. Therefore, wish for all beings to be free from suffering and the causes and conditions of suffering.

Realize that you yourself fail to appreciate suffering. It makes you fearful, depressed, desperate, and anguished, and you want to get rid of it as soon as possible. This is also the response of every other sentient being. So why not realize that all beings are equal in their wish to eliminate suffering and the causes of suffering? Repeat this prayer again and again,

> May all beings be free from suffering and the causes of suffering.

Think about some minor suffering you might experience, such as a headache or a small burn on your finger, and the fact that all other beings have the same cares, concerns, and attachments. And then think about beings undergoing immense physical suffering—beings who are butchered, roasted, chopped up while still alive, boiled, burnt, or killed by weapons.

Or think about beings who are ill. Just as there are degrees of illness, so are there degrees of pain. Bring all this suffering into your own experience. Forget that they are others, and experience this suffering as if it were your own. How intensely would you long to be free of suffering? How desperate, depressed, anguished or fearful would you feel? What would be your motivation in these circumstances?

So this is what we do as we meditate. We wish for the suffering of all sentient beings to be eliminated. We wish for them all to be free from suffering and from the causes and conditions of suffering, from both dormant karmic seeds and from the manifest karma that has come to fruition through causes and conditions. Wishing for all sentient beings to be free, repeat this wish again and again.

When you yourself suffer, suffering is not an intellectual thing. Realize that the suffering of beings is real. Therefore wish all beings to be free from all kinds of suffering, without any bias towards or against any particular type of suffering. Repeat your prayer over and over again.

Remember that all these beings have been your mother, protecting you from suffering and the causes of suffering. From birth onwards, they saved you from your own vulnerability to suffering. They transcended all limitations in order to find ways of protecting you. They gave you their life's energy and resources, their physical, mental, and emotional strength. Each and every one of them has been your parent at some point.

Right now, when they are in so much pain and suffering, how dare you forget them? How could you? It would be incredibly callous, incredibly ignoble, to ignore their pain. Wish for all of them to be free from suffering and the causes of suffering, even more strongly than you wish for yourself. If you cannot manage that, at least make your wish equal to what you would wish for yourself.

Then reflect on your own suffering, on how self-absorbed you are, twenty-four hours a day; how concerned, unhappy, depressed, and fearful you are. Think how, in a larger context, your suffering is insignificant, and yet you are completely trapped and absorbed in it. Think about how embarrassing that is.

And then consider how much you need to develop kindness and compassion and the wish for all beings to be free from suffering and the causes of suffering.

Realize that the attainment of buddhahood depends on compassionate mind. It is the very essence of *bodhichitta;* it is the heart of all the buddhas and bodhisattvas. The realization of the paths and *bhumis* and all the benefits of that realization depend upon *bodhichitta. Bodhichitta* in its very essence is compassion. What a boon it would be to develop genuine compassion, the authentic wish for all beings to be free from suffering and the causes of suffering! Repeat this wish over and over again.

Also consider how wonderful it would be to liberate yourself from self-absorption. The only way to do this is to develop compassion. The only way to eliminate the pain of being absorbed in your own concerns, of turning a small amount of suffering into something huge inside your mind, is to develop the genuine compassion that transcends self-absorption.

And then wish all beings may be free from suffering and the causes of suffering. Repeat the line again and again,

May all beings be free from suffering and the causes of suffering.

As you recite this prayer, realize that all suffering is relative. Relative to the suffering of others, your suffering is small, so try to forget your suffering. Your focus is on the suffering of all, so wish for all beings to be free from suffering and the causes and conditions of suffering.

Pray to the buddhas that you may develop genuine compassion, a longing and concern for the suffering of all beings, a longing for all of them to be free from the immediate experience of suffering and the conditional experience that is to come.

Pray to the bodhisattvas. Vow to follow, embrace, and cultivate their compassionate heart.

Sympathetic Joy

NEXT, THINK OF SOMEONE who is happy and of whom you are jealous. How could you be jealous because somebody else is happy?

Since your aim is to develop *bodhichitta*, loving-kindness, compassion, and a good heart, how could you possibly be jealous?

Instead, inspire yourself to be genuinely happy that both you and this other person have obtained the causes and conditions of happiness, whatever the cause of the other person's joy.

Consider the other person's joy as if it were your own achievement, and rejoice from deep within your heart, without the slightest hint of jealousy. Completely overcome your jealousy. See how jealousy ruins your attempts at cultivating a kind and compassionate heart and universal, supreme *bodhichitta*.

It is in fact extremely rare for someone to obtain the causes and conditions of happiness and be really happy in samsara. So when this does happen, it is far more appropriate to rejoice than to be jealous and condemnatory. Therefore, rejoice from deep within your heart.

Remember that all these beings are your parents. When they are happy, you can rejoice. Think of how all sentient beings are exactly the same as you. When you are happy, you must enjoy and appreciate your happiness, as it is the result of your merit. In the same way, when somebody else is happy, they must enjoy their happiness, because it is the result of their merit. So what is the point of being jealous? How unnatural and ignoble jealousy is!

Therefore, rejoice deeply, with a pure heart. Rejoice with a fresh mind, and embrace other people's happiness as if it were your own. Since there is really no difference between you and other sentient beings, rejoice in other people's achievements as if they were your own.

Then rejoice in the achievements of the supreme beings, the buddhas and bodhisattvas. Rejoice in the freedom that they have gained and the noble qualities that they have achieved.

Whenever you hear any good news, rejoice; whenever you see or come to know about something that is good, rejoice, rather than being jealous or neutral.

Rejoice without a trace of indifference or jealousy, as if the achievement were your own or that of a mother sentient being whom you love. Then repeat the third line of the prayer again and again,

May all never be separated from the great happiness devoid of suffering.

Wishing them all to attain more and more happiness, continue to recite the prayer.

Equanimity

REALIZE THAT YOU must develop loving-kindness, compassion, and sympathetic joy in equal measure towards all beings. Every sentient being has been your parent and is in the same situation as you. Every sentient being desires to be happy, wants to obtain the causes and conditions of happiness, and desires to be free from suffering and the causes and conditions of suffering.

Because there is not even a single way in which you are different from other sentient beings in this regard, you must develop equanimity towards all beings. Passion, aggression, and ignorance blind us to this deep connection. Remember that life changes. Throughout your past lives, into the present one and on into the future ones, our relationships, feelings, love, care, and compassion all change if they are based on ignorance.

As passion and aggression are not reliable, you must develop equanimity in relation to loving-kindness, compassion, and sympathetic joy. These qualities are based on something real, something that is untainted by passion, aggression, and ignorance. These qualities are based on relying on all sentient beings as if they were your mother and father, as they all have been. Regarding yourself and others as equal, wish for all sentient beings to be happy and free from suffering.

Then, reflect on the fact that we are all deluded. In reality, samsara and suffering truly do not exist. They are only a delusion and a dream, and we are all bound to that delusion.

Therefore, on the basis of the four immeasurables, wish that all mother sentient beings might obtain freedom from the delusion of samsara and suffering. May they obtain the true nirvana of the innate enlightened *dharmakaya*.

Student: How do we cultivate generosity?

Rinpoche: It is difficult to shake up and loosen the core of the ego unless you part from something that is precious to you, something that you cling to. Therefore we need to make offerings. Often we make offerings with good intentions, but our actions are controlled and calculated. Since we never really let go of our deepest attachments, they stay unchanged. For us to become worthy so that *bodhichitta* dawns within, we need to release our own deepest attachments.

During Atisha's visit to Tibet, when one group of people requested and received the bodhisattva vow, Atisha asked them to make a great offering. The first offering they made was not good enough, so he said that they needed to make a greater offering. Again, they made an even greater offering to the Three Jewels, and again he said that it was not good enough. Three times he made them increase their offering. It's quite likely that they had to stretch themselves and make a dent in their resources. That was exactly the point—to have people feel that they were parting from their deepest attachments. What they got in return was freedom.

Receiving the bodhisattva vow is being given freedom. It is when pure intention takes birth inside of you. You are not getting anything back other than that. You need to envision that freedom and pure intention being born inside you, and sense how that can sustain while your deepest attachments cannot. You need to be really interested in doing this. If you are not quite clear and are haphazardly trying to take the vow, it will simply be mere ritual. If you truly seek freedom and the pure intention of an altruistic mind to sustain you, then give birth to aspiration *bodhichitta*. If you no longer want things and attachments to nourish you—which they never do anyway—then you need to take this seriously. Without giving up your attachments, merely thinking, "I am going to imagine all of this," and making an offering does not shake the core of your selfishness. Your attachments are going to be right there, just like a hard rock at the bottom of the river. You need to realistically shake up your attachments, and beyond that, extend the offerings with your imagination as well. Patrul Rinpoche mentions that when we make imagined offerings, we do not need to have a clear picture of them; rather, we must just have a flash of them and offer them with a pure heart.

When discussing the bodhisattva vow, it must be clear that we are not getting anything back in terms of material gain. We are not even aiming to gain merit. We are simply aiming to get the freedom that is lacking inside of us. To be truly free, the pure altruistic mind must come alive inside us. Not everyone has the capacity to envision freedom and the pure intention of altruistic mind as a support that can sustain their mind. To even be able to imagine that freedom, we need to have a lot of merit. It is not a matter of merely imagining it, but also of having interest, which shows further merit from previous lifetimes. In addition to this merit from past lives, giving offerings and taking vows in the present life can be really beneficial. What we are doing now leaves an imprint so that perhaps in future lives we can do it more fully.

One good reason to practice making offerings to the Three Jewels is that, in the beginning, we tend to want something back. This is just an aspect of ordinary mind and the ordinary mind's habit. We may be looking for material things, health, spiritual gain, or realization. The mind tends to go in that direction. Without this kind of initial expectation, it can be too difficult to let go of that slick-looking green thing and turn it into food or butter lamps or whatever. Actually, in reality, if you truly look at it, this slick green thing is nothing other than our projection of worth or value. Due to the mind's habit and the feeling of attachment, there is a consensual value placed on money.

It is very natural for people to think of getting something in return. But actually, as you offer more, you begin to want less for yourself. You come to make offerings out of an appreciation for freedom, and you loosen your need for what can come back to you. Not needing or wanting anything is the greatest freedom. Without this, we may have the mind of a trader, giving one thing for something else in return.

Regardless of all this, by making offerings there will be merit. Dedicate it to those who are actually in need, those who actually want and cling to things. You will see your own mind transforming through this process. This is a great experience to have—

observing how your mind was before, how your mind is in the middle, and how your mind is in the end.

Ask anyone which would be better, absolute freedom or a return on an offering. Anyone who thinks about it would have to say freedom. It is an amazing feeling to not have any kind of clinging or attachment to what we offer. However, in reality, it takes a lot of merit to get to that point. Only when we make offerings as large as possible can we experience that. It's a catch-22: You have to offer to get there. It's hard to imagine what that would be like, yet this is what we should all aim towards. In future lives we will get to that place of not having any need whatsoever, but still being able to make many offerings to the Three Jewels and do so much good in the world for others. Right now we can only engender the appreciation for this free state of mind.

At present, it is okay to stay where you are and give what you can as an offering. Still, make sure that this ultimately leads to freedom. If your mind includes the possibility of this freedom, you will eventually get it. If you do not imagine that freedom and do not embrace it as part of your merit and the result of generosity, then you will not get it. Instead you will always be materializing gold and silver; generosity will not lead into mental and emotional freedom. Therefore, when making any offering, even the smallest; make it an offering that directs us to total freedom from all material things, free from clinging even to spiritual things. Aim for freedom from *all* clinging.

This is a great prayer and a good thing to envision for ourselves, since we are all bound by attachment to the material world. It is our attachments that get us stuck—our own mind and emotions. The Buddhist way is the ability to see the weaknesses in one's own mind and to not feel discouraged, but rather to feel inspired to get beyond them. That is the only way we can actually make a bridge from where we are now to where we want to be. There is merit in looking at our bondage and weaknesses, even though at this point we are unable to completely leave them behind. Sometimes it is helpful to imagine how it would be if we could actually get rid of the bondage of our strong attachment. Imagining in this way opens the door of our mind so that we can truly get there. Offering is the first approach.

Rejoice

IN THE CONTEXT of ordinary life, one of the most difficult things is to actually rejoice in another's good fortune. If somebody we like or love is fortunate, we may manage to squeeze out some appreciation—but forget about being happy with our enemies' good fortune! Honestly, though, rejoicing practice is incredible. It offers a great deal of benefit for very little effort.

A saying goes, "Little labor, much gain." On the path of Dharma, less effort and greater benefit is a sign of wisdom. This principle applies even in technology! Less effort combined with greater efficiency and productivity signals progress. Take the example of computers. When I first came to the West, computers were huge. Now they are small and streamlined—much better than those old big ones. Efficiency has been established.

In the case of the path, this is also true. There is the path to be reborn in the higher realms, and then the path of Hinayana. Next is the path of Mahayana, and lastly that of Vajrayana. In the Vajrayana there are many levels of the path. Studying these, you will see how in the higher *yanas* there is less effort and greater productivity because there is more wisdom. The degree of wisdom corresponds to how much you gain through relatively little effort. Not that I am anti labor, but if you don't have to, why bother?

Rejoicing practice involves modest labor with a tremendous gain. Before we actually practice rejoicing, we must be able to appreciate the merit of others as equal to our own. In order to do that, we must lose some of our dualistic thinking regarding merit, as in, "It's mine; it's others'." More specifically, we tend to think that if something is "mine," no matter how insignificant it is, it has to be good. If it belongs to others, the thought tends to be, "However momentous it might be, it's still not good." We have to be able to resolve this misguided mental attitude. If we can actually get to the point where, in the context of the practice of *bodhichitta*, we give up our lives and possessions as well as "our" merit for the enlightenment of all beings and for their security and freedom, we will be able to let go of our self-importance. Then we can easily get to the point of rejoicing in others' merit, being able to praise others' merit with tremendous sincerity and a genuine heart.

A story tells about a day when the Buddha was invited by his father. He and the monks were offered an enormous amount of delicious food for lunch. An old beggar lady who saw this thought to herself, "Because of past merit, this man has been born as a king. To be able to do such things now—how incredibly fortunate for him! In the future he will have even more merit." From the depths of her heart, she rejoiced in his actions. She didn't feel there was any competition—she just felt pure appreciation for him and what he was doing. At the end of the day the Buddha asked his father, "Should I dedicate the merit of this for you, or for someone who has gained even more merit than you today?" The king replied, "Please dedicate it to whoever has gained the most merit." And the Buddha dedicated the merit to the old beggar woman.

When you have no arrogance, no degree of competitiveness, and when you are able to appreciate and see the significance of the positive actions of others, you can rejoice a great deal. But feeling competitiveness inside yourself—a sense of arrogance or of holding on to the self—reduces the opportunity to rejoice. Having no sense of clinging to the self, no arrogance or competitive feelings at all, opens up your mind to truly and fully rejoice. This kind of practice provides a great opportunity for people who have less to not feel competitive and to gain the same amount of merit by freely rejoicing in others' merit. The ability to appreciate others' good qualities and good deeds depends on how psychologically free you are from arrogance, pride, competitiveness, and any sense of deprivation. When you are free of these, you have the opportunity to actually fully rejoice. Not only do you gain merit; you will become free of troubles. This is incredible.

To exercise conscious rejoicing is an amazing practice, particularly for those of us who often feel we are lacking something in our lives. We may not know how to pinpoint what we lack, but when someone else says, "I have this," or, "I have that," the feeling arises that we are missing out on the goodies. To hear about someone's good luck can actually become painful. This shows that our covetous mind is caught in dissatisfaction and a poverty mentality. It shows a lack of merit. Rejoicing practice is the best way to reverse that.

Anytime you hear about someone else's good fortune, you can practice appreciating the achievements, qualities, and wealth of others. Appreciate them exactly as if they were yours. Even if you could somehow have the whole world, you might still feel it was not enough. Especially in regard to your own possessions, you can only get a finite amount of happiness out of them. But by rejoicing in others having them, the joy becomes unlimited. Through this practice you can constantly be happy and have a tremendous sense of cheerfulness. It's like this: A king can only have a limited amount of wealth in his treasure house compared to how much his subjects can own collectively. The king who rejoices in all his subjects becoming as rich as a king would actually have much greater happiness than the king who simply focused on his own wealth.

The opportunity to be sustained by your good heart, your good wishes for others, and your sense of rejoicing in others' positive qualities, positive conduct, and merit is limitless. Not only do you have the joy and happiness that comes from that, you can also have more or at least equal merit. If somebody does meritorious work, there may be resources that are not so clean involved in that. The individual who rejoices in that merit doesn't know about this, however, so the rejoicing itself is pure, and thus even greater. The person who goes through the trouble of doing the action may even get less merit than the person rejoicing. This clearly illustrates how rejoicing in merit is a great practice for all of us.

In our current age, there is a great deal of competitiveness and feeling internally impoverished. Many people's hearts lack richness. People feel squeezed. In the old days, having one gold coin made a person feel rich; nowadays, having a hundred gold coins does not make a person that rich. People feel that no matter how much wealth they have, it is not enough. This has something to do with the era and time. The feeling of impoverishment is strong in everyone's psychological makeup. Perhaps this could be remedied by rejoicing. When you rejoice, you really feel like you have richness inside. Your good heart sustains your mind.

At the very least, rejoicing practice will let you be unperturbed when you hear good things about others. This in itself is a great freedom. Investigate how other people respond when they hear about good things happening to someone else or about others' qualities or gains. Quite often there's a sense of almost wanting to turn away from hearing this news, an uneasiness. But if the gain is theirs or associated with them in some way, there is delight in their response. This shows that we in these small ways are very restricted by our minds, to not be able to truly embrace the goodness in the world. We have to be able to at least appreciate the goodness in the world, even if it's in the hands of our enemy. Mature people in the old days had an appreciation of an enemy's good qualities. The practitioner's way is to be able to appreciate all and have no enemies, to treat everyone's achievements as if they were one's own and to rejoice in their goodness.

You hear so many great stories. Somebody is building a 108-foot-tall Guru Rinpoche statue, while someone else is building a great stupa or a big monastery, or a lama is supporting and honoring many monks. If you can rejoice in these great deeds, you can actually earn all of that merit too. It really doesn't have to be happening here on "my property"; it doesn't have to be "my doing," "my this," or "my that." That's a very limited perspective. If you're starting something, that's wonderful. But if you aren't starting something, that doesn't mean that you can't rejoice and have a tremendous sense of appreciation of the fact that somebody else is doing it.

I very much request you all to consider rejoicing as a practice that can shape our psychology and our sense of contentment. It helps us get over our own lack of appreciation of the world and the goodness in it. By rejoicing, we can truly be on the side of virtue. If we are not appreciating somebody who is doing virtue, then we are on the side of non-virtue. To be on the side of virtue is to rejoice in it regardless of who performs the deeds. In this way, rejoicing can benefit us all tremendously. Virtue is rare these days, and when it occurs we must rise to appreciate it and rejoice in it. This can involve any level from an individual on up to a community. Rejoice fully in all positive efforts made to benefit beings, the Dharma, and the environment. Rejoicing in others' qualities is contagious; we will also want to have those qualities. In order to magnetize others' good qualities, first be appreciative, rejoice in their qualities, and do not feel inferior.

Jealousy is merely a matter of embarrassment about your own state of mind. Getting jealous and covering it up—as in calling jealous speech "discernment" is just like carefully putting icing on a piece of shit. When you are jealous about something, you say, "It's not so good as it is; it's not wholesome as it is; it has a problem. You have not understood the problem. Only I have understood the problem, and I am going to give you a lesson about what the problem is. And you should actually pay heed to me." But in reality it's very obvious that you are speaking out of jealousy, and that you yourself are feeling quite embarrassed. People are looking at you, nodding, and knowing what's going on. You cannot successfully put icing on shit. It just becomes a total loss of face.

Jealousy offers us a great opportunity to rejoice. However often we are jealous becomes that many opportunities to cleanse ourselves of this negative pattern. Here's a practice to do: Identify people you are jealous of. Think, "Whom do I have jealousy towards? Whom do I actually tend to pick on out of my jealousy?" Then sit down and, one by one, practice rejoicing and cleanse your mind. After that kind of practice, the next time the person's name comes up, your face will light up instead of darkening.

Right after you rejoice, dedicate the merit. Whether it is your own merit or that of others, you could actually rejoice in the merit and dedicate that over and over. Constantly rejoicing and dedicating could be your main practice.

Student: I have a problem rejoicing. What more can I do?

Rinpoche: People work so hard to obtain conventional happiness. If they never got anything out of that, it would all be for nothing. To wish for them to have some fruit of their labor, and then to rejoice in those who actually have some fruit, is a decent thing to do. It's not necessarily that you believe this is ultimate happiness, or that you actually believe this is happiness with no side effects or problems. Still, consider how hard people strive, look at these great cities, New York, San Francisco or Los Angeles, where people rush around like ants, caught up in the speed and trying to get here and there. Basically they are actually trying to have some accomplishment of tainted happiness. And tainted happiness as *we* know from our own experience, is like salty water: The more you drink, the thirstier you get. That's just the way it is, unless you have some self-reflection, some detachment and understanding of your true nature. The more wealth you obtain, the more greed increases. The more power you gain, the larger your appetite for power grows. The more leisure you have, the more self-indulgent you become.

Many of our psychological and emotional problems nowadays seem to be because of two things. One is because there is a sense of, let's say, the Hollywood or television version of how things should be. This involves a tremendous dissatisfaction and an internal feeling of impoverishment. People see an image on the screen and think, "Why is life not like that for me?" There is a chronic sense of internal complaining about one's life, the feeling that one is missing out on the cheese or being deprived of the American dream as it is ideally presented by media. The second aspect is that there is always dissatisfaction from a little bit of jealousy or envy. This is a big problem. Actually if you visit another country where there is not much television, where there are not so many prefabricated ideas of how our lives should be—of how things should be according to Hollywood's point of view—people may have very little, but they are quite content with that. And there is also not so much resentment towards others who have it. There is a sense of, "Oh, so-and-so is wealthy," but it comes with a kind of appreciation for his or her good merit.

You also have to think about karma and merit in regard to this subject. So many people put tremendous effort into doing things to make themselves successful, but they never are. And then here comes someone else who's not really putting much of an effort into it and becomes wealthy right away. This kind of example shows that effort alone is not the thing. Part of it comes from one's previous karma and merit. When you do not include this factor in the equation, your mind can be a little discontented with life. You think your life is not good enough; it should be better. You resent others and feel jealous. But in reality, nobody gets even an extra penny without his or her own karma and merit being involved. Similarly, nobody suffers the lack of anything without his or her own karma and merit being involved. From the perspective of merit and karma, nobody is lucky and nobody is unlucky.

There's no such thing as lucky and unlucky in Buddhist termi-
nology. It's all due to past lives, all the way up to this particular life.
People have to tune in to practicing merit. Therefore, you want to
wish the best to those whose actions are about to bear fruit—to
rejoice in them, and likewise you want to wish the best to people
who are putting a great deal of effort and time into getting some
fruit. You want to rejoice with them too. You see how farmers work
so hard to cultivate a crop, what they go through day and night.
If you were to wish these farmers not to have a good crop, that
would simply be indecent—mean, in fact. If you see somebody
who worked hard and got the crop they wanted, you should be
happy. Wish that the farmer who is working hard will eventually
reap a great crop. Be happy for whoever is happy. Towards those
who are discontented, wish that their fate be changed.

From this point of view, wishing happiness for others is more
motivated by pity at seeing how people work so hard in samsara
to gain this tainted happiness that doesn't last very long. Do not
focus so much on the problematic sides of it. If you focus on the
problems, not only might you not find happiness in samsara, you
might not find happiness in nirvana either! Happiness is a relative thing, and it is dualistic.

Student: There's a practical question about a technique a few
of us discussed yesterday at lunch. When we try to reflect on a
situation, often times that which we reflect on becomes a story
and we get lost in it rather than doing the reflection. So, could
you give advice about techniques for reflecting without that—
knowing how to reflect on actual situations without getting lost
in the story?

Rinpoche: Your question is how to be objective in your reflection, right? I think the way to do this is to try to become a

researcher yourself—to find the real truth, the real story, rather than a bias towards your own tendency to see it one way or the other. If you become a researcher searching out the truth, the real story, rather than creating a bias out of your own inclinations to support somebody and be against someone else or even be in support of the Dharma and against samsara, you will not become partial. If you become a genuine researcher, you are trying to find the truth. Then the Dharma and your findings will come together. And this is the way to be objective. And you have to take time. Not everything becomes clear [*Snaps fingers*] at once. You have to take time too to sometimes sit with the situation or sit with what you are contemplating to find out more.

Let's say, for instance, that something is said in the Dharma about how your mind works. And then you are contemplating whether your mind is working that way or not. Maybe you don't see very clearly that your mind works that way. But then let's say you are in pain, in the pain of feeling quite jealous about something. At that point, if you could disassociate yourself from the pain and look at the pain more closely and openly, you would see that what the Dharma says about your state of mind much clearer. Pain can be a better revealer of your own mind than any other state. Sometimes pain is really a great ally for you to discover certain defects in your mind. Pain sometimes can serve as an illuminator. People think, "Oh, I'm not very arrogant; I don't feel so arrogant; I don't think I see myself as arrogant." And it's true, people feel that way. But when they are offended and they have pain, they can see how they have been arrogant all along. My answer to you is, "Become a researcher," and not just in support of the Dharma. That is why Buddha has said,

"Examine my words like a goldsmith examines gold; do not take my word because it's my word." These words encourage us to become like a researcher. Use pain to get to know your state of mind much more deeply, in order to develop a conviction in the Dharma.

Digesting Pain

PRIMARILY, WE FEEL, we act on are our instincts. When we truly contemplate this situation, we have to acknowledge that these are not all natural instincts, because some of them lead us against our fundamental innate desire to be happy. Not only do they lead us against it, but also they actually bring us suffering. Obviously there are some flaws in these instincts! If they were natural, primordially pure instincts, they would not have any flaws.

These instincts are shaped and conditioned by the ignorant confusion of believing that there is a self and that that self is extremely important. To cling, cherish, and protect the self is a state of mind that has been with us for so long it feels completely natural—you might say instinctual. But if these were genuine, natural instincts, we could never get rid of them. If that were the case, nobody would be able to get enlightened. Precisely because there are so many individuals who have already become enlightened, we can say that self-clinging is not a truly natural, primordial instinct.

It's not always good to fight against instincts. When we have a dualistic battle with them we can become quite discouraged and despondent, because they are so ingrained in our psyche. So, instead of dualistically battling with them, transform them.

Transform them skillfully with wisdom. The way to do this is to actually change the focus from ourselves to all others. Cherish others as we cherish ourselves; protect others as we protect ourselves, and by using our tendency to cherish and protect, our loving-kindness and compassion will increase. In doing this, we reverse the entire psychology without giving up working within the context of sentient mind.

These are the specific, great methods of the Mahayana teachings. Through them, what you experienced in the beginning as a problem later becomes an asset. It is also realistic, because if you had no experience of how to love, to imagine loving is very difficult. But if you have some understanding of how to love someone, even if it is yourself, then it is easy to love others as well. Basically you just change the focus. Maybe you do not do so immediately, but gradually. You can't stop making yourself the focus right away; it takes a long time to completely undo the habit that we all have. But if you actually practice, then slowly, slowly it changes. When you see the wisdom of doing such a thing for oneself and others—when that wisdom dawns much more clearly in your mind—you will naturally follow its lead. The habit becomes weaker and weaker.

When wisdom has not dawned clearly in us, this habit has much more power over us. When wisdom dawns within us, however, habit loses its grip. This is a process, rather than a leap of faith or intention. In this way we can all feel encouraged that whatever we are doing, a little practice of *bodhichitta* will eventually lead us somewhere, as long as we don't give it up. This is also a safe path. If we try to leap, expecting to get there right away, it is difficult. We have a saying in Tibetan: "If a fox tries to leap the distance a lion can jump, the fox will break his back." We have to be realistic. The point is not to get there immediately. The point is to cover the distance. If we proceed in this way, disappointment with ourselves and despondency over the lack of result in the practice will not arise.

Especially endeavor to integrate practice with our confusion and our afflicting emotions that create pain and suffering for us. To do this, we have to study and understand our confusion—really sit and examine our confusion and conflicting emotions, getting to know them and recognizing how they don't serve us.

This is not always an easy thing to do. Usually the problem we have is not being able to sit with them, because a certain amount of pain is involved and we react against the pain and try to escape. We have to change that pattern. If we want to sit with our confusion, if we want to sit with our conflicting emotions, if we want to study and understand them more intimately, we have to be able to tolerate a certain degree of pain. Pain is actually the great doorway to self-reflection. Without the pain we may have no reason to engage in self-reflection, or we may forget to do it even if we want to. By using pain as a doorway to self-reflection, we will find out a lot about our own mind and the way it is—both how it is functions and how it is dysfunctional.

Sit with and meditate on your mind to get a greater sense of freedom from negative habits and to gain more trust and confidence in its positive aspects. You will progress, depending on your merit and diligence, and increase your loving-kindness, compassion, sympathetic joy, and equanimity. If you have even a tinge of noble qualities, and you give your word to somebody, saying, "OK, I will do this for you," you will either do it, try your best to do it, or at least feel some concern for not being able to follow your word if you fail in the attempt. It is very rare that basically good people will act completely irresponsibly or shame-lessly and not keep their word. Everyone has some conscience. Everyone has some sense of dignity. Everyone has some sense of individual pride and some pinch of wanting to do what they say they will do, some desire to mean what they say.

When you are actually seriously contemplating cultivating the four immeasurables of loving-kindness, compassion, sympa-thetic joy, and equanimity and you recite the lines, the next time you act in a way that goes against that you will feel a little bit of hesitation. You will feel a little bit like you should follow your words, thoughts, and intention. That is a good start. That is the beginning of practice. As time goes on, you will see how those heartfelt feelings are extended to others, how they cleanse, secure, and bring your mind to another level of happiness. Naturally you will walk towards that.

Becoming a practitioner is based on how interested we grow to be in this process. At first we are not a practitioner; we are completely governed by habit. The mind of a practitioner begins as we train in the opposite and grow to be more reliable. Our mind becomes steadfast in our sanity and begins to serve us the way we intend it to do so. Prior to that we were not stable because our minds were not stable. Mind was tumultuous, torturing us. But this is no longer the case. This kind of transformation is the true significance and meaning of becoming a practitioner, a student of the Dharma.

Without Dharma, as I said, we are like a fly fruitlessly trying to escape and hitting his head against a window. We resort to our own confusion, which does not provide us with any way out. I'm sure we all feel this sometimes. When we try to figure things out, our minds spinning and spinning, we get nowhere. The fear is actually making us more distressed. We are like that fly, exhausting ourselves and dying. Humans not only jeopardize themselves in this state; they jeopardize others as well.

In the Dharma there is a view. When there is a view, there is wisdom. When there is wisdom, there must be skillful means to apprehend that wisdom, which can be applied by individuals interested in practice. We need to simply rise to the occasion. We have to tolerate pain. If we have zero tolerance to pain, we will panic and forget to look into what we can do. The way to really become a practitioner is to have the courage to tolerate relative pain. There is no absolute pain. All relative pain must be tolerated with courage and an understanding that we can end the pain. We do so by first tolerating it, then figuring out the causes and conditions of it and reversing these causes and conditions.

We all know that we can bear physical pain. People sometimes even like physical pain, which is why they work out hard at the gym or climb Mount Everest. They actually bear physical pain quite well—but not mental, emotional pain. Mental pain is confusion itself, not knowing what to do. Emotional pain is feeling hurt. If you really look at who is hurt, *nobody* is hurt, since there is no self to hurt! It is only the mind that has gotten into this place where it feels hurt.

We try desperately to not experience this hurt or pain. When we realize there is no one to be hurt, only the mind imagining it is hurt, then the desperation is diffused, as it is recognized to be pointless. Everything passes; this feeling of hurt will also pass. We don't need to act prematurely to get rid of it—even if we did, it might make it worse instead of better. This feeling of hurt or emotional pain interdependently originates with the self being there as someone to be hurt. The mind projects the self being offended and hurt, the mind conjures up the feeling of hurt, and then the mind also says, "It's unreasonable; I can't bear this! I need to patch this right away! I can't stay one minute longer in this pain!" Of course, for someone who is not a practitioner there is a legitimate pain and hurt, because one believes totally in the self and the experience of the self being wronged. The pain and hurt are real and unbearable. There is a real desperation to feel healed.

As practitioners, we should train in seeing how all of this happens in the relative, as an illusion. Since it is all happening relatively, we shouldn't take it completely seriously. It's like how actors train. They go through the motions, but in actuality they know they are actors playing a role. It's not real. We should start to see things that way.

Do not believe in the absolute, truly existing self, in mind, or in projections of the mind. The pain, the frustrations and desperations—none of these really exist. This is not merely hypothetical. When we have a glimpse of the nature of mind, we'll know that all this play doesn't truly exist. The insubstantiality of mind becomes our own true experience.

As you become more mentally focused and aware, you will not act out of habit and you will no longer become desperate and vulnerable. Simply summon up your courage to sit still, to be present, and practice whatever practice you do to penetrate to the core of your confusion. By doing this you can see that one minute you are in total misery and the next minute the misery has vanished. Your mind's situation is temporary, transitory, and empty. Nothing is intrinsic: If it were, these moods would last forever, but they clearly do not.

Through practice, you can overcome the pain. At first, you become desperate so quickly. You throw in the towel so easily, like one of those guys in the boxing ring, and say, "I can't do it." Walking out of the ring is one thing, but with only your own mind involved, you cannot walk out on it. Where are you going to go? What are you going to actually achieve from that?

You have to be able to sit with your experience and tolerate it, to learn to let things pass. Immediately jumping into practice to kill the pain doesn't work either, because of your desperation to remedy the pain. The pain doesn't even have time to blossom. By leaping into practice, you are too attached to the cessation of pain. Acting out of fear never works, and practice used dualistically, like water on fire, is not that effective. Summon up your courage to let the pain fade away by itself. To enhance that process, practice.

I would encourage you to tolerate and find value in your pain in this way. Use your pain as a doorway to deep self-reflection regarding what you know about the Dharma. Become silent, and turn your attention inside; get centered, and become clear. It's as if you had the skill to be a great marathon runner, but your own mind overwhelmed you to such a degree that you couldn't even race with a child. In these situations you fall under the power of confusion, which only gets worse by the minute. It is helpful to become silent and centered. In any kind of ordinary situation, when you lose your balance you have to get it back. Mentally you have to regain your poise as a practitioner. Expecting to have poise all the time is unrealistic. You are bound to lose your composure on occasion, and then the only question is how do you get it back.

What helps this process the most is your faith in your own ability as a practitioner—your faith in yourself. Where does that faith come from? It comes from the strength of your intention.

The more you have the burning intention to become a practitioner, the more you will have faith in your ability to become a genuine practitioner. Moreover, your faith in the practice of Dharma will increase. Dharma practice is what all the *tathagatas* of the past have done so efficiently, and it worked for them.

When our yearning is merely lukewarm and our interest in practice is haphazard, our faith is undermined by our attitude. Even if we have faith, our interest doesn't support it completely, so faith is not able to come in strongly in our time of need. When the interest and the yearning are there, strong faith intensifies. Belief and devotion strengthen. When devotion, faith, and the belief in the experience of being able to transform our mind by the skillful means of the *tathagatas* become a reality, it is not even a matter of faith any more. It is our experience, our life, and our own truth at that point. Confusion simply falls away.

I myself have trouble tolerating emotional pain, but I increasingly see how we must welcome our pain in order to become strong, stable, and capable of establishing ourselves as practitioners. We need to summon our courage to tolerate more pain in many different ways. Often, people think that tolerance means something like, "Grin and bear it." Perhaps for just a little bit in the beginning there is an element of this, but from that point on tolerance is actually about becoming clear inside.

Use your view, your understanding, to allow the negative experience to actually dissolve by itself without putting more fuel on it. Apply your clear mind and intention. Work with your own understanding of the interdependent origination of how this pain has come to exist and how in reality it doesn't exist, how it is just the play of illusion. In this way, even tolerance is not the right word. The phrase is more like "eat your pain." When you eat it and digest it, metabolize it, it becomes nourishing. It's no longer much of a problem. It's like the metaphor of a peacock eating poison, transforming that which can harm into that which heals.

Get to know the pain more intimately. Getting to know your own pain intimately can make you revolt against the root cause that created the pain in the first place. Of course you always feel the pain, but *knowing* the pain intimately is different from feeling the pain. Knowing the pain intimately means using discriminating awareness, discriminating intelligence. Feel the pain—even animals feel the pain. In working with knowing, you have to sit with your pain. You have to very objectively get into your pain to understand your pain more and then inspire yourself to be patient in order to work with it further.

Studying the problem first and then making a bridge to the practices that remedy it is a great Mahayana method for increasing *paramita* practice in your life. The only drawback is that often when you do this, a sense of discouragement or judgment of your own mind may show up. When this kind of aversion or nausea towards yourself arises, know that something positive is happening. Something is penetrating to the core. If you give in to it and quit, nothing will happen. The habit will stay intact. But if you don't give in to it, if you simply continue your practice without giving in to these reactions, slowly the reactions will be overcome and you will not be so judgmental of yourself. You will find yourself thinking more intelligently, being more spacious with your own mind, tendencies, and habits. You will think about your habits from a different perspective, and this will be very good. When you know how to think about your own habits from a very objective viewpoint—when you are spacious with your own tendencies and don't have unrealistic expectations for yourself—you will find a greater sense of peace and contentment within yourself right there and then, even though you may still have a lot of bad habits. So it's very good to sit with your mind and study it in light of the four immeasurables, in light of altruistic mind, in light of the six *paramitas.*

Lastly, I want to say that people need the taste of peace, of joy, of freedom, of power, of a clear mind, of a contented mind, of being deeply in harmony with one's mind, in order to sustain themselves on the path. If there is no integration of these qualities, if there is only self-hate and self-reproach, it doesn't happen. There has to be an appreciation of one's positive side as well as one's negative side. The positive side has to get stronger, edging out the negative side, rather than completely rejecting the negative side or not even knowing what it is.

This whole dualistic tendency is the biggest problem of a practitioner's life. It's not because the teachings are taught in that way or that the path is that way, but rather because it's how we relate to everything in the world. We relate in a dualistic way, so that when we come to the path, when we come to the Dharma, we relate to our obscurations in a negative way and get aggressive with ourselves.

In actuality, the potential is very beautiful. It's very beautiful in that you can have room for it all. You can actually have a dance with the habits, and you can actually slowly and firmly get ahead of your habits, outsmart your habits. In order to outsmart your habits, you need to know your habits. When you are in a blind state, the tricks played on you by your habits and weaknesses can get you. But if you are not blind, they have no way to hook you. If you don't study those blind spots and do research on them, it's very difficult to outsmart your habits. Sometimes a big blessing can come, and then all of a sudden you get some kind of breakthrough. Usually, though, it's very hard to get some kind of leverage with your habits. That's why it's good to treat our most negative and bothersome habits as a subject of study and research.

Integration

THE DEFINITION OF A SENTIENT BEING is to have a mind that experiences pain and pleasure, suffering and happiness. As I mentioned previously, we humans all unconditionally desire happiness and freedom from pain. Likewise, in the animal realm, the instinct is also to seek happiness and freedom from suffering. However, animals are limited in their pursuit of this due to their inability to think clearly and act positively. In the human realm we have the critical intelligence that animals lack.

Human beings have the ability to discern what is true happiness and what is not. We can understand the causes of happiness and reject the causes of suffering. Even though we as humans possess this capacity for discrimination, it remains dormant if we don't use it. To be able to use this ability, we need to cultivate the three wisdoms. With the hearing wisdom, the contemplative wisdom, and the meditative wisdom, the natural aptitude we have can be brought out to the fullest extent to serve our most basic needs.

We must acknowledge our potential and capacity. If we fail to do so, we degrade ourselves to the level of animals. Demeaning ourselves is a common problem. Saying, "Oh, I can't do this," is actually a form of laziness. "Oh, it's beyond me. I can't think. It's too much pressure to think." Things like this keep us stuck at a lower level of intelligence, unable to develop our potential. First you must acknowledge your critical intelligence and how it needs to be trained and developed.

Next, endeavor to comprehend true happiness, which has a wide range. There are two kinds of happiness: sensory pleasure and mental happiness. Sensory pleasure is when you see, hear, smell, taste, or experience something wonderful—music being played, a nice perfume, a scented flower, tasty food, the feeling of being warm and comfortable, or coolness on a hot day. Mental happiness is much more subtle. Pleasurable physical sensations can only be created through objects that have the capacity to give you gratification. But who is the true experiencer of this happiness? Although sensory perception is experienced, the pleasure is in the discriminative mind. It's the inner mind that truly experiences this contentment, this pleasure. When the inner mind is totally stressed and worried about something, the pleasures surrounding the sensory body, like being in a beautiful house or a nice garden, do not give rise to mental ease. Mind is depressed. Mind is worried. This inner mind that is in pain dominates the experience and outshines the sensory pleasures that are being fed to the sensory organs.

Most of the time happiness depends on its own resource, the inner mind. The inner mind has a constant dialogue going on within itself, depending upon your view, perspective, and attitude. It is this inner mind that shapes one's ability to find deep happiness and strength. That's where the Dharma comes in. The Dharma is not going to provide you with anything for the sensory body. Dharma is all food for the inner mind. Dharma provides you with the view, perspective, and attitudes to train yourself and discipline this inner mind. Dharma guides you to bring out your positive qualities and eliminate your negative characteristics. If you really want happiness, you have to first discern the kind of happiness you want. If you want sensory pleasure, then Dharma does not have much to offer you. If you want happiness of mind, however, then Dharma has a lot to offer.

In our current condition, we have no consistent happiness. What is the problem? From my point of view, and I have really drawn a strict conclusion on this matter, it is because we lack the practice of *bodhichitta*—we are unaware of the practice of *bodhichitta*. If we gain a knowledge and awareness of the practice of *bodhichitta*, we will be able to follow through on that longing to be free from suffering and be happy. The more we engage in *bodhichitta* practice, the stronger the blessing of the practice will be in our lives. If that practice of *bodhichitta* is not there, it is very difficult to be free from suffering and to sustain our mind in true, uncommon happiness.

We have two states of mind: relative mind and the absolute state of mind, which is enlightened. Ultimately, there is no difference between an enlightened being's nature and that of a sentient being. Realization of the enlightened nature is one way to fulfill the longing all sentient beings have to be happy and free from suffering. Through realization we can actually transform all our perceptions, thoughts, and emotions and attain the state of freedom, happiness, and bliss.

Having this longing for happiness motivates us to eventually establish it. Fueled by the power of this longing, we should generate the aspiration *bodhichitta* and not give up the wish to be free. When the realization of that wish is completely stabilized, we can interact with the world like so many of the great practitioners of the past. But in our lifetime, for us to feel that strong renunciation is difficult; also, the circumstances of our lives don't always allow us to do that easily. Still, we shouldn't give up the desire to become a genuine practitioner. The reason to become a genuine practitioner is to fully understand the wisdom of the Buddha's enlightened teachings and to be able to integrate our mind with them for the benefit of all beings. To do this, we first need to purify our mind in the correct ways. Next, we need to establish our mind in the state of happiness that comes from practicing the Buddha's teachings. Finally, we have to have the wish to benefit others as much as we can. The practice of *bodhichitta* makes that possible.

We are trying to verify that which needs to be purified. We do not want to purify anything and everything, but rather something that harms and hurts us over and over again. We seek to purify something that we can actually verify, not only once, but again and again and again with our critical intelligence.

That which truly harms us is anger of all types—big, medium, small, gross, subtle—and all kinds of attachment, jealousy, competitiveness, and pride. The ultimate maker of all these negative emotions is stupidity. If we were wise and had no trace of stupidity, we wouldn't get so involved in negative emotions. We wouldn't be so hooked by these emotions. The motor that runs all of these emotions is stupidity itself—ignorance. This is the fifth disturbing emotion. These five, attachment, jealousy, competiveness, pride and stupidity are negative because they cause use to experience the harm and pain that result from our mind being in an unhealthy state. This is what needs to be purified. Imagine a future without any attachment, aggression, jealousy, competitiveness, or arrogance. Our mind is going to be quite pure. Our mind is going to be quite peaceful. Our mind is going to be quite free.

We have to aim our mind towards being that way. We have to see the possibility for something like that to happen in our mind by taking the support of the Buddha's teaching. If we remedy the root, the symptoms are naturally cured. That root, according to the Buddha's teachings, is nothing other than our self-importance. Our self-importance brings up these five negative emotions throughout the day and long into the night. Imagine having a good practice to remedy this self-importance, so it is not out of control. And then slowly, slowly get to a point where the self-importance is realized to be a thing designated by mind. In reality, there is no self to be found. And then have a deeper sense of true wisdom to remedy the self-importance, a realization of selflessness, the state of enlightened mind.

The initial stages of purification are very simple and easy to understand. We can all identify how much we have suffered from our own attachment, jealousy, pride, ignorance, and aggression. There is no reason to deny or dispute this, although in the midst of an attack by these emotions, we might defend or justify them. Later, when we regain our sanity and have some wisdom to fall back on—not simply going with the emotions or indulging the emotions—we will be able to admit the suffering that has been created. We would never call it sane to indulge in our surging emotions and be carried away by deluded behavior. The time when we are sane is when we actually have some wisdom to fall back on in self-reflection, so that we can see what actually hurt us, how it hurt us, and what could have been avoided, what we could have done differently.

No matter how we are trained, as a philosopher or a practitioner, there are times when we are insane. But still, there are times we are sane. Otherwise everybody would have to be admitted to the mental hospital, and that would be too much of an expense for the state and federal governments! The times when we are sane are when we have wisdom to fall back on. During those times, we want to practice the Dharma, learn the essence of the Buddha's wisdom, apply the enlightened teachings to our mind, and actually change. We want to change this random insanity, unpredictability, and dependence on outer circumstances that create the situation for our mind to react in terms of the five afflicting emotions. That we do not have control over outer circumstances makes our state of mind unpredictable in a negative way. If somebody says something that is hurtful, we react. This makes our life very unstable. We are shaky all the time, and to a degree, we are insane. And we want to change that.

To try to change that, we must get hold of our mind in a particular way. A lot of people try to control their rage, attachment, jealousy, and pride, but somehow the emotions get out of control. We know these emotions are not good, that these emotions are not helpful, and that they hurt others and us. We want to try to hold them back, but we don't know how to get a proper grip on them. Mind, with its emotional energy, is not something we can easily seize. A concrete object, even a hot iron ball, can be held in our hands, given proper mantras and training. Workers building the Empire State Building actually threw hot iron from one hand to the other.

We can do that with physical objects, but with the mind it's not so simple. Basically, there is no possibility of holding our mind without embracing it with wisdom. We have to give the mind something to do that is opposite to how it normally reacts or uses its energy. Unless we have the wisdom to counteract the habitual power of the mind that is making us react in a particular direction, that habit actually can become much more explosive and difficult.

We are talking through all this on the level of thought, on the emotional level. We must have some wisdom that actually guides the mind from the wrong habitual pattern to a new one, creating a new habit. Without this, it's very difficult for the mind to control itself. And that's why we have hopeless cases. We never learn from life; we only wear ourselves out. And then maybe we get some freedom. But if we have to wear ourselves out to get some freedom, it is almost impossible to wait for all the neuroses to wear themselves out.

To try to hold your mind—to suppress the temptations and seeds of temptation that are ripening within the disturbing emotions—is disastrous. It simply doesn't work. Mind at that point needs to know what it should do. What would be the best thing for mind to do when it gets angry, for instance? Use the energy of anger to fuel kindness. That you can do, because you know anger is not good. Anger harms you, and it harms others. You do not necessarily want to get angry. One who follows anger is powerless. So, be really convinced that being kind will remedy this anger. Generate kind thoughts and feelings—this you have to learn from Dharma. But once you have learned it, you can do it.

Kindness and angry thoughts cannot exist together. One will always overpower the other. If you examine the competition between anger and kindness, which will win in the end? People tend to say, "Oh, maybe the anger will be much stronger." That's only because of bad habit, however. If you don't have that habit, if your habit is not that way, anger has no reason to win, because it doesn't do any good to you or anyone else. It harms you, and it harms others too. Anger is based on ignorance, based on actually having no self-control. All those points make the anger fundamentally weak. Kindness, on the other hand, does good for you and others. You know that already. It remedies anger by freeing you from it and from the sensation of it. Kindness based on practice is self-willed. For all these reasons, kindness will win out over anger.

If you have habitually indulged in anger for a long time, of course, that might give it added power. But in objective terms, anger has no reason to win out over kindness, while kindness has all sorts of reasons to win out over anger, as does sympathetic joy over jealousy. If you don't practice and want to continuously indulge, well, that is another story. But if you practice, sympathetic joy has many reasons to win out over jealousy, just as detachment has much more reason to win out over attachment, as does humbleness over arrogance and pride. All the practices of the four immeasurables and positive qualities have solid, genuine, real reasons to win. And this is your capital. Right? If you don't know your own capital, you can never actually increase your wealth. You have to know what your capital is in order for your wealth to increase. The practices of *bodhichitta* that you try to cultivate have all the reasons to win over that which you want your mind to be free from.

To do that, to free your mind is to learn through the hearing and contemplative wisdoms and to put them into practice through meditation. The application aspect is important here. Merely reading a medical text is not going to cure you of a disease, is it? You have to not only read it, but also do what the text suggests. You have to put the instructions into practice. From my point of view—and this is from the point of view of the teachings, too—you have a great chance to free yourself from the five negative disturbing emotions, day by day, week by week, and month by month. There can come a time when you will have no negative emotions in your mind from morning till night, and eventually not even in your dreams. What makes this happen is the practice of *bodhichitta,* the practice of the genuine four immeasurables. Based on the practice of the four immeasurables, generate the real and genuine wish to be enlightened for the benefit of others. This is not just an ordinary wish, but a deep and heartfelt desire that all beings be free from the suffering produced by the five disturbing emotions.

This is not an abstract thing. Our own suffering is very clear. We want to be free from suffering, not only for ourselves, but also for all beings. We want to attain the state of mind's perfect health—complete realization of its own absolute and relative potentials, with the perfect bliss that comes with it. If there is no bliss in the realization of absolute truth and in the full blossoming of the potential of the relative positive qualities, what's the point? There is bliss in realization. Although it's non-dual, it's still blissful. We want that kind of freedom for all sentient beings, as well as for ourselves.

It's not like chanting by rote, when we have no time to think what we are saying. Now we know what enlightenment is. It is not theoretical. Now, with this wish—for all beings to be enlightened—strong inside of us, nothing else can occupy our mind. This wish comes up in our thoughts; it is a deep, burning flame inside of our heart. Thoughts come and go, but the burning is there all the time. Yearning for enlightenment is there all the time.

In the past, perhaps the yearning for happiness and freedom was there, but it didn't have a broad aim. Maybe the yearning only focused on the self. This time it's not focused on yourself, it's focused on all beings, everyone. That much is different. In the past, you did not know true, uncommon happiness. Now you know what happiness is. In the past, you did not know what freedom was. Now you do. In the past, you did not know what caused suffering. Now you know. In the past, you did not know how to get happiness. Now you do. In some ways it's the same, but in another way it is not, and that makes all the difference. Very simply, there is a very big change inside of you. That yearning is burning as it always has, but now it's united with the aim to be free from suffering: knowing what suffering is, what the cause of suffering is, and wishing happiness not merely for yourself but for all beings, to have the happiness that is enlightenment.

What can bring uncommon happiness to you is wishing that others be happy. Wishing that others be happy, wishing others to be enlightened, and dedicating your whole life to the practice of the *paramitas*, which actually engages in the work of enlightenment, is what brings you there.

Bodhichitta practice brings you to that ultimate happiness. This time, something is different. You were on the wrong track in the past, but now you are on the right track. Being able to discriminate between the two with your intelligence is a big improvement. In the past you longed for freedom and happiness only for yourself, and that put you on the wrong track. Longing for freedom and wishing for happiness is good, because that's needed. There's no harm in that. But wishing that only for yourself puts you on the wrong track. It is not only you who is in need of freedom and happiness. The need here is all-pervasive, because all sentient beings need this, so you direct your focus towards them as well. Focusing only on yourself in the past led you astray. Now, longing for all beings to be free from suffering and wishing all beings to be happy and perfectly enlightened is the right track.

How do you know that this was the wrong track and that you are now on the right track? When you wished only for you own happiness, you never got it. Instead, it made things worse. But wishing all beings to be free from suffering and wishing all beings to be happy is how all of the buddhas and bodhisattvas became enlightened.

If you want happiness for yourself, practice kindness—you will be happy. If you practice attachment, you will suffer. If you practice compassion, you will be happy. If you practice aggression, you will be unhappy. From your own life experience you can see the evidence and feel quite encouraged to go in the right direction. When you yearn from deep within not only for yourself, but for all beings, to be free from suffering and have happiness that gets translated into wishing all beings to be free from the sufferings of samsara and to be enlightened. Occupy your mind with that and making those prayers—then nothing can attack you. There is no way for the negative emotions to strike. You have secured your mind completely. It is impossible for negative emotions to arise while you are practicing *bodhichitta*. While there is sunlight, it is impossible for darkness to come.

As long as you are practicing *bodhichitta*, how can negative emotions attack you? Only when your mind leaves *bodhichitta* practice and gets back into old habits, into its usual pattern, can your mind be attacked. This life, this day-to-day, week-to-week, month-to-month affair of your whole life, is where you must secure your mind. If you truly secure your mind, there is no way for it to be attacked by the afflicting emotions. Compare the power of your newly learned *bodhichitta* practice with the power of countless aeons of various births with all their negative habits. Which is more powerful? The newly learned practice is much more powerful than anything else.

Feel encouraged. This is the capital that will secure your mind through the practice of *bodhichitta*. Never second-guess what supports you the best. The more convinced and clear you are inside, the greater the practitioner you will become. If you are second-guessing, doubting, not quite sure what supports you the most—wondering if you want this support for sure—it will take a long time to mature. Eventually you will mature, but in the process you will be quite abused by all the negative emotions. The sooner you settle your mind on this, the quicker you will be able to secure your mind in the practice of *bodhichitta*.

Additionally, there won't be such a contest between wisdom and ignorance. Right now we are still somewhat relying on ignorance. When we pit wisdom against ignorance, wisdom has already won. We only have to fight against habit. In the deepest analysis, we have no real conflict here, but only a conflict in the power of habits, which is easy to remedy. When habits challenge us, we can take them on. However, we can't take ignorance on all by ourselves and win.

The first step is to get as clear as possible. Gain conviction in the wisdom of the Dharma, in the practice of the Dharma, as the remedy that supports you. Do not second-guess yourself, have doubts, or remain unsure. If the challenge of the habitual tendencies comes, you can take them on. That can actually be exciting, since you have no confusion. It's a way you can actually measure your growth. Everyone wants to grow, so it can be exciting. The more habitual power you can overcome, the more exciting it gets. Removing fundamental ignorance is the most important thing. Your own experience removes that ignorance. You yourself are the best teacher of all. Your own experience teaches you what supports you and what doesn't, what makes sense and what doesn't, what enlightens you and what makes you stay in the same dark ignorant place.

From all of our experiences, we can discern that what the Buddha taught and what sentient beings experience are not different things. It's proven that the five negative afflicting emotions harm us, hurt us, and bring us down constantly, day by day, hour by hour. The primary cause of that is self-importance. What can actually remedy the five negative disturbing emotions? The practice of the four immeasurables, and particularly a wish for all beings to be free from suffering and happy—this wish being translated into a wish for the enlightenment of all beings. That yearning for all beings to be enlightened, making that a prayer and keeping that yearning and praying going all the time, is aspiration *bodhichitta*. That deep wish for oneself to be enlightened for the benefit of all beings secures your mind. The negative emotions cannot attack you when this is present. Only habit can attack you. And the frequency and success with which habits attack you are a measure of your growth. This can be exciting. It's not like you are always going to win. You might have some regrets here and there. But basically you will win. You could bet on this, unlike on a soccer game, which could go one way or the other. Here you can bet, because there's no danger of losing in the long run.

This is really the essence of the Buddha's teachings, the essence of the practice. This is what you will learn. Try it out. From tonight until tomorrow morning, right before you fall asleep, or right after you wake up, or simply continuously, make this yearning for freedom inside of you—yearn for all beings to be free from suffering. Make this wish inside of you for all beings to be happy, and translate that into the wish for enlightenment for all beings. Keep this wish throughout the night and day; see how your mind is sustained in a state of peace and bliss and is subsequently protected and secured from negativity. That alone is evidence, and will make you more convinced.

Aspiration and Engagement

AS I MENTIONED EARLIER, *bodhichitta* has two aspects: aspiration and engagement. Aspiration *bodhichitta* consists of first generating loving-kindness, compassion, and sympathetic joy, and then extending that to all mother sentient beings without excluding anyone. Ultimate happiness and its cause—ultimate freedom from suffering and its cause—are nothing other than perfect enlightenment. Enlightenment is defined as perfect happiness and freedom. To wish all beings may have happiness and freedom from suffering is none other than wishing beings to be enlightened. With this purpose in mind, you yourself need to be enlightened so that you can truly work on freeing beings from suffering and bringing them to perfect happiness. If you are not enlightened, you lack the wisdom, the skillful means, the knowledge, the power, in other words, everything that really works, to bring beings out of the suffering of samsara and guide them to the path to enlightenment. Therefore, you need to become enlightened first so that you can have the wisdom, love, and power to bring all the other sentient beings to enlightenment.

This makes perfect sense. If two people are drowning in quicksand, one cannot pull the other out. The wish to be enlightened yourself does not arise out of selfishness. It is not because you believe that getting enlightened will exclusively free you from suffering. It realistically works out for the better for all. Your wish to be enlightened for the sake of all sentient beings' enlightenment is nothing other than aspiration *bodhichitta*.

Now, engagement *bodhichitta* goes beyond wishing to actually embark on the path of enlightenment. It starts with the practice of purifying your obscurations and goes all the way up to obtaining the qualities of enlightenment. To engage in the practices of the six *paramitas* is known as engagement *bodhichitta*. It is just like someone wishing to go to Lhasa and then traveling on the road. The wishing is the aspiration *bodhichitta*, while the traveling is the engagement *bodhichitta*. Moreover, wishing to be enlightened for the benefit of all beings but not taking the bodhisattva vow is aspiration *bodhichitta*. However, taking the vow and then right after starting to practice the six *paramitas* is engagement *bodhichitta*.

We have already established that all beings desire happiness and freedom from suffering. Since there is no difference between yourself and others in this regard, try removing yourself from the center of your prayers or any spiritual practices that you do and instead put all mother sentient beings in the center. Think of making prayers, studying, and practicing on the spiritual path as a labor on behalf of mother sentient beings for their perfect happiness and freedom from suffering. Dedicate yourself to be a complete servant of mother sentient beings. Put yourself in the lowest position. In fact, you are actually raising yourself to become totally free of self-centeredness and to become very noble and endowed with the qualities of realization of enlightened mind.

In the Kadampa tradition there are three slogans: "Leave the human circle. Enter the circle of dogs. Then you will obtain the divine state." Leaving the human world means leaving all the ego battles that you have with yourself and consequently with others. You completely give up clinging to the self with the intention to become free of this. So you consider yourself as the lowest of all low human beings, not even human. You might as well be comfortable among dogs; simply enter into dogdom. However at the same time, naturally, you are getting rid of self-centeredness and the conceited mind that binds you to samsara; therefore, as soon as it is abandoned, you rise into the position of being divine. This is all in relation to the practice of truly removing yourself from the center of all of your prayers, all of your practices, all of your efforts to be on the path to enlightenment, and slowly aiming to benefit all mother sentient beings by your prayers, your practice, and your involvement in the spiritual path.

Within engagement *bodhichitta* there are two subdivisions: the relative engagement and absolute engagement practices. The relative practices are generosity, patience, discipline, diligence, and meditation. The absolute practice is the meditation on *prajñaparamita*.

In this context I will explain the two types of happiness: compounded and uncompounded. Compounded happiness is when you meditate on loving-kindness and your mind becomes free of ordinary neuroses, such as anger. You are getting rid of the anger and instilling loving-kindness in your mind. Positive energy flows out of the meditation and touches your state of mind. Compounded happiness is cultivated: it is created by causes and conditions. This is relative happiness.

Now, what is uncompounded happiness? It is resting in the absolute truth. Recognize that your absolute nature is free of all delusion. Realize that your absolute nature is pregnant with all positive qualities; then discover a sense of delight in that. You are not working hard to cultivate and apply causes and conditions. You are simply resting in your own primordial nature, in emptiness. Emptiness is not a void, like an empty room. It has a vibrant luminosity that is self-aware of the nature itself. This state of mind is very agile. With it, you can actually know how to apply and understand the causes and conditions that lead to certain kinds of fruition and what the path can be. This whole idea is that the nature of mind is not something that you cultivate. It's simply there; all you do is try to appreciate that. Resting in the nature of mind is primordial happiness, the natural inheritance of all beings. Relative happiness always falls short of complete happiness. With absolute, uncompounded happiness there is a sense of deep satisfaction.

In the practice of Dharma we train in the relative happiness of mind. We learn how to cultivate happiness through loving-kindness, compassion, sympathetic joy, and equanimity. We cultivate an altruistic mind, the wish to benefit all beings, to bring all beings to a perfect state of happiness along with its causes and conditions, and to perfect the state of freedom from suffering and its causes and conditions. Training in all of these increases the relative happiness inside our mind. We do this by suppressing the old habits of ego and then training in generosity, in discipline, in patience, in diligence, in meditation, and in wisdom. These all increase relative happiness, inner mind's happiness.

On the other hand, we also try to meditate on the absolute nature, and this is more profound: It is training ourselves to fully embody our own disposition—enlightened mind—and to have a sense of it, an experience of it, not only in a hypothetical way but in a real and experiential way. While living in samsara, in the midst of the suffering experienced by others, the bodhisattva is not subject to the suffering in the same way as confused sentient beings are. The uncompounded happiness is the absolute *bodhichitta* practice. Relative compounded happiness is the relative *bodhichitta* practice. Both of these are a great medicine that heals the minds of sentient beings, steeped in ignorance, steeped in the afflictive emotions, steeped in grasping to a self that cannot actually be found, and steeped also in the delusions that karma has produced.

If these two medicines, the practices of ultimate and relative *bodhichitta*, don't interact with and penetrate our ordinary state of mind, then our mind will remain as it is. Since there is no merging of the medicines with our mind, there is no perfect result. To merge them, we need to appreciate both. We need to appreciate anger as well as patience, stinginess as well as generosity. We can't be too hostile towards aggression, as if aggression is an absolute. We need to say, "Okay. I am getting angry here. I am in the pain of anger, and this is actually an opportunity for me to apply patience and get rid of this pain by the strength of patience. Through patience I have the opportunity to interact with my anger and eliminate it." To do this we need to study both sides—both the illness and the medicine. Whether or not the medicine affects the illness depends on how great the understanding of the illness is. So, in all this we are provided with enormous opportunities to appreciate pain, as well as the cessation of pain and the happiness that the practice provides.

Student: When you say remove ourselves from our prayers, do you mean completely from our prayers or just from the center?

Rinpoche: If you can remove yourself completely, that would be good. The experience of removing yourself from the center of your prayers and any involvement in your spiritual studies and practice is not a bad bargain. It has a very good outcome, if you do not cling to that outcome. Clinging actually gets in the way. You need to work with lifetimes of habits of clinging to self and aiming to benefit that self during any and every activity. So removing yourself means two things. Mentally always engaging in mother sentient beings' mind and giving up any benefits to them. Along with this is letting go of any habits that you may have of clinging to the self and replacing the clinging with feelings of loving-kindness and compassion towards all mother sentient beings

Let's say that you are working for a big company. If you do your job well, you will get a big commission. There are two ways to do this. One way is to think about the commission and work from that perspective. The other is to think only about the job and to work from there. Let me suggest that you do your spiritual practices and training by thinking about the job to be done, not about the commission—even though there is most definitely a commission. The commission is the freedom that you get inside, the purification you begin to experience. Just think about all mother sentient beings, generate the aspiration to benefit them, and in the end dedicate the merit. By practicing in this way, the purification that takes place is the commission. Once the purification takes place, the qualities of enlightenment begin to surface. These emerging qualities have certain functions and benefits, such as the benefit for others.

Let's correlate the work example with the three *kayas.* The *dharmakaya* is one's own commission, while the *sambhogakaya* and *nirmanakaya* are for the benefit of all others. It will not work if you think, "I want to attain *dharmakaya*." That "I" itself hinders you from obtaining *dharmakaya*. *Dharmakaya* must be obtained by the motivation to benefit others.

The purity of the wish to obtain enlightenment depends on two things: to what degree we have gotten rid of self-centeredness, and to what degree we are able to generate loving-kindness and compassion for others. Cleansing our mind also helps us to generate loving-kindness towards others, as it lessens self-centeredness. The result is always to have the completely selfless wish to bring all beings to enlightenment. To have that wish blazing in our heart is a practice inclusive of the four immeasurables. Getting rid of self-centeredness is like finding a treasure in our mind, a wish-fulfilling jewel. This pure wish is protection from all the usual delusions and egoistic problems. All the buddhas and bodhisattvas that have ever gained enlightenment were born from that wish to benefit others. That wish was kept continuously in their hearts; it never died out. Slowly and gradually it purified their remaining obscurations and gathered all the merits of positive qualities, so that they became enlightened.

Enlightenment starts from that first thought, which is compounded. Since it is compounded, it is something that dies out by itself because it is generated. As every thought arises, it dissolves. As every compounded thing arises, it dissolves. When you keep the continuum of that thought, the whole chain of thoughts strengthens until enlightenment. In the beginning you might have to generate the sense of loving-kindness and compassion with some effort and really work hard to get rid of any self-centeredness in your thoughts of loving-kindness and compassion. But over time, as it is strengthened, the effort required is less and less. Eventually it arises on its own in your mind, and at that point it contains the depth of that loving-kindness and compassion as well. The self-centeredness is not so present.

The wish to be enlightened for the benefit of all mother sentient beings changes over time. It is not the wish itself that changes, but the quality of the wish changes tremendously. In the beginning the wish is not that authentic. It's feeble and relatively easily destroyed by unfavorable circumstances. That wish, however much intended to be genuine, may still hold a tinge of self-centeredness. In your loving-kindness and compassion that is extended to all beings, there may be a subtle level of unconsciously thinking about how to benefit yourself. By continuously practicing that wish over time, selfishness is brought to the surface and exhausted through the power of the training. The wish becomes more authentic and genuine, as loving-kindness, compassion, and sympathetic joy become very real and instinctive.

This is not only the case with *bodhichitta* practice—it is the case with anything. For instance, when you learn a subject, after a while, you don't have to spend as much time to truly know it. At some point, you master what you have studied. You became adept, and that subject becomes instinctive.

In essence, you are trying to strengthen aspiration *bodhichitta* in the continuum of your mind. You will not be able to do this if you expect the *bodhichitta* wish to come about without practice. If it merely depends on your mood, it will not happen. Aspiration *bodhichitta* has to be practiced. Many people have trouble getting onto the cushion and practicing regularly. In that situation, it might be helpful to think: "This is a time-away from my own self-importance." The way to enact this change of attitude is to do a *bodhichitta* practice—to actually generate *bodhichitta* to cleanse your self-importance.

Now, if someone has not understood what self-importance is and how it gets in the way of true happiness, then I can understand how they would not even be interested in being a Dharma practitioner in the first place. To be a Dharma practitioner you have to really acknowledge the shortcomings of self-importance. We, as Dharma practitioners, have acknowledged how self-importance prevents us from enjoying our lives, our days, and even our moments, let alone anything beyond that.

Here is another example to support this. At some point during the day, people think it's time to take a shower. It's almost a necessity nowadays for people to take a shower each day. Some people are very delighted to take a shower in the morning just as they get up. People take a shower because they want to feel fresh, cleansed, and to have some feeling of dignity. Similarly, if we acknowledge how self-importance consistently prevents us from enjoying our life, our days, and our moments, then it makes sense to really cleanse our self-importance. To cleanse our self-importance, we must do *bodhichitta* practice every day. If we think in this way, we will feel more inspired to be regular in the path. Taking a shower freshens up our body. *Bodhichitta* practice freshens up our mind.

The main thing to address when doing practice is to do it with your mind present. Do not practice distractedly. This type of practice becomes work, and work without an objective or any achievement is a burden and a pressure. Try to practice in as precise a way as possible. At least be sure that your practice is aimed at benefiting others. Intend to cleanse your own self-importance. At the moment your mind is disturbed, you must cleanse it. When the objective of cleansing your mind of its self-importance is coupled with the aim to benefit others, even for just thirty minutes or an hour of practice every day, it will sustain you throughout the day. Maybe you will truly see the reasons to do even more practice to sustain yourself. Possibly you will have a greater feeling of *bodhichitta* supporting you, and a greater level of joy.

I never thought this way before that practice could be regarded as an obligation, until some students expressed this to me. However, when practice becomes an obligation or a pressure, then we don't know why we are doing it. Even if we know why, it doesn't necessarily reduce our self-importance, but adds to it. Maybe our practice has a goal, but if the goal is self-importance, that becomes a problem. We should aim to cleanse our self-importance, and see the necessity of cleansing our mind in the same way that we see the necessity of cleansing our body. Just as we see we need to brush our teeth, we should see the need to brush our mind.

If someone is not in agreement with the Buddhist teachings, has no faith in working with self-importance, and doesn't even see self-importance as a problem, then maybe that is a whole different thing. But if we believe the Buddha's teachings and his words regarding the problems of self-importance, then we should at least be as diligent in practice as we are in taking a shower. How long does a shower take—fifteen or twenty minutes? What about those lavish showers that take half an hour to an hour? Or even brushing our teeth—how long does that take? It takes about two minutes with Oral-B.

Similarly, we need to cleanse our mind with *bodhichitta*. Do so every morning, before plunging into prayers, practice, or meditation. Think about how this deep motivation for the benefit of others could cleanse our self-importance. Practice with some awareness, and examine whether it works or not. If it works, rejoice. If it is not working, see what is not working and remedy that.

Student: In relation to the poisons, I was wondering if you could address the wisdoms a little bit more?

Rinpoche: My view is that mind is naturally endowed with certain qualities, such as being able to love, care, and feel compassion. If these qualities of mind are looked upon as confusion, as useless, then we can never put them into use. Unfortunately these qualities of mind have gotten mixed up with ignorance and the by-product of ignorance, the belief in the self. When the qualities of mind are guided by wisdom, then that wisdom serves beings, enabling us to appreciate our own natural inheritance and directing us to the path of enlightenment.

The question arises that since there is no truly existing self, how can one imagine others to actually exist? When someone attains egolessness or enlightenment, that individual realizes that the self doesn't exist. That person can see other people's delusion in terms of their strong belief that the self does exist and their corresponding clinging to that idea. Since there are always going to be deluded, miserable beings who believe the self does exist, there is endless potential to use these qualities of mind, of the *bodhi* heart—the love, care, compassion, wisdom, power, and so on—to serve beings. The wisdom here is that even though one realizes that ultimately nirvana is the state of mind absent of all duality and delusion, these relative positive qualities of mind can still be used on the path to serve suffering beings endlessly.

For instance, take the example of loving your child. Having that experience gives you an even greater opportunity to love someone else. Perhaps the problem we have in loving our own children is that there is self-centeredness. Still, this ability to love, the loving itself, is not the problem. This ability gives you a great deal of information about how to love others. If you try to teach love to a robot it is impossible, because the robot doesn't have a mind. Since intelligent mind is present in sentient beings and in particular in human beings, it can be shaped in the right direction so as to use the qualities that are inherent to it. There is much advantage in being human. This is the viewpoint of the wisdom of the Mahayana.

Stepping Stones: The Six Paramitas

TO REITERATE, ASPIRATION *bodhichitta* is the genuine, sincere, and deep wish to attain enlightenment for the benefit of all sentient beings. Aspiration *bodhichitta* is our intention to go somewhere, like traveling to San Francisco. Engagement *bodhichitta* is the follow-up after the intention has been generated. It is being involved—engaging our body, speech, and mind in the practice of the *paramitas*, which are generosity, discipline, patience, diligence, meditation, and wisdom. That's like getting into the car and driving to San Francisco.

Engagement *bodhichitta* can be divided into relative and absolute practice. The relative practice accumulates relative merit, while the absolute practice accumulates wisdom. Generosity, discipline, patience, diligence, and meditation are all relative practices. Relative practice involves our body, speech, and mind, particularly the mind, as ordinary thoughts and feelings are transformed by practice.

This is easy to manage, because our thoughts and feelings are controlled and manipulated by our habitual patterns. These habitual patterns are based on our own tendency to engage in the five disturbing emotions of passion, aggression, stupidity, jealousy, and pride, and whatever mixtures of these emotions that may arise. Those emotions ultimately come from cherishing and protecting the self. In answering the question, what is the self that we are grasping, and do we see this self when we grasp? We can say that most probably no one will actually see the self. People can identify grasping to the self, but never see the self itself. That's very ironic, isn't it—the way we grasp at the self as if there is one, but never see it.

Regardless of this irony, there is definitely a belief that there is a self, and there's also a belief that this self has certain characteristics. A primary belief regarding the characteristics of self is that it is singular. This self is also believed to be permanent. It is permanent in the sense that the one who was born forty-two years ago and the one who I am now are considered to be the same person. Or that yesterday's me and today's me are the same. The one who did something and the one who actually experienced the result of that are considered to be the same person, good or bad.

We also believe the self to be intrinsic. There's no thought of the self being dependent on causes and conditions. We think that self exists without causes and conditions. We don't see the self like a rainbow, which appears as a result of moisture and sunshine coming together in the environment. Instead, we see this self as solid. If somebody says mean things, the self gets hurt. If somebody says something nice, the self gets happy. It's not unresponsive. It is conscious, and this capacity to experience fuels the pain and the happiness in a seemingly tangible way. We say, "my body," "my speech," and "my mind." On these occasions the self is seen as an owner of body, speech, and mind. On other occasions we see the body, speech, or mind as the self: "I see, I hear, I feel."

There are a lot of assumptions being made about the self. But has anybody seen the true existence of this self? To actually see the self, it must exist within the *skandhas* or within the body, speech, and mind. If you examine the body, speech, and mind— the perceptions, feelings, thoughts, and consciousness—you will never find anything that is singular. Everything has many parts. This body is made of billions and trillions of particles, and those particles in turn are made of particles. Examining deeply, you will not find anything other than emptiness. It is similar with speech: Paragraphs are made of sentences, sentences are made of words, words are made of syllables, and syllables are made of sounds. When you investigate like this, in the end, it is an empty void. There is nothing you can say is truly existent.

With regard to the mind in general, there are perceptions, feelings, thoughts, and consciousness. There are many different aspects to the mind. All of these continuously rise and cease. If you look closely, there's nothing in the body, speech, or mind that is a singular thing existing intrinsically, by itself, without causes and conditions. Because everything exists due to causes and conditions, they are changing as they arise, remain, and cease. On a subtle level, they are continuously changing. On the coarse level, you see gross change.

We actually designate a self to exist. The designator is the ignorant mind. But if we really do a thorough search, we will never find the self as we assume it to be. The *skandhas*[2] do exist in the relative sense. They exist in the relative sense with many, many parts to each, not as a singular entity. Also, they exist through causes and conditions. Nothing exists without causes and conditions. And anything that exists due to causes and conditions is going to be impermanent. As it arises, it has to fall.

Anything that is created by causes and conditions, that rises and ceases simultaneously, does not truly exist. This is how a continuum starts—a moment arises that is subsequent to the first, which has already arisen and ceased. It looks just like the first moment, but it's not. And then a third arises after the second that looks like the second but is not, and so on. There is a gap between all three; otherwise, they would become one. The primary cause for the second one to come into existence is the first. The primary cause for the third one to come into existence is the second. If you try to actually find the origin, you will never find it—it's infinite. Between each of those three, there's a gap. They are in no way linked or connected. In reality, when you examine causes and conditions, they only seemingly and functionally exist. You will never be able to locate a cause producing an effect, nor a linear connection between the effect and the cause.

Causes and conditions are more or less illusory. Effect is illusory. Illusory refers to something that seemingly does exist, but, when you really look closely, there's nothing substantial, nothing there as a reality with any characteristics. In this way, everything is relative. The relative is always illusory. The nature of relative appearances is always going to be *shunyata*. Examining this carefully, you find no substantial, intrinsic, singular, permanent thing in the entire phenomenal world. There's just the mere appearance of causes and conditions coming together and producing a manifestation. Cause itself is empty of inherent existence, effect itself is empty, the relation between cause and effect is empty, and the appearance of anything is empty.

The entire phenomenal world is nothing other than empty appearance. It is not how we believe it to be—singular, permanent, intrinsic, and solid. That is ignorant mind's designation of things. Ignorant mind's strong insistence that things are really like that, and its holding on to that assumption for so long with such conviction, have an effect in terms of our mistaken perception. But the phenomenal world is always nothing other than empty appearance. In the mind, the subtlest appearance experienced is the first rising of thoughts. In the phenomenal world, there's emptiness. In the mind, there's emptiness. Between the emptiness of the table and the emptiness of the mind, there is no differentiation.

All appearance is empty, and everything is impermanent. You can see this in your mind as well as in a particular phenomenon. It's a little more difficult to see this in a phenomenon in terms of perception, but with wisdom mind, you can. At some point, when you refine your perception, you can actually see in this way. But it takes a while for the perceptions to be able to see how the atoms of this table are simultaneously arising and ceasing. It's easier to see how in the mind a thought arises and ceases simultaneously. Beyond the subtlest rising, there's only emptiness. That we can see.

Beyond the arising, dwelling, and ceasing is emptiness. Everything is emptiness, but that doesn't mean a void. There's an awareness of the empty quality that is luminous as well. You can actually see emptiness as your own nature. In the case of the self, that means there's no appearance of the self. There's only an absence of what you have projected based on the *skandhas*, which are relative. Relative appearance and what your ignorant mind has projected, a truly existing self, are totally opposite to the actual truth.

Now the projection comes to light to be seen exactly as it is— there's nothing there. Take the example of projecting a rope to be a snake. You never see the snake; you only see the rope, right? The characteristics of the rope and the snake are completely different. When you realize this, the projection is understood as complete illusion. Similarly, you come to see that the phenomenal world by nature is empty but still has appearance; that appearance is relative truth. What you have projected as a truly existing self is also seen to be delusion, because that appearance of the self and the characteristics of the appearance of the self are totally opposite.

In that way, you have the dawn of realization. Our self is always an ignorant mind projecting a self to exist in the *skandhas,* as an owner, as a reality, which it is not. Seeing through this is the realization of the egolessness of the self. Now, realizing how the *skandhas* themselves are, in the ultimate sense, nothing other than empty and luminous—that realization—is called egolessness of dharmas. Egolessness of dharmas is a much greater than realization egolessness of the self.

Egolessness of the self is realizing that the self does not exist either absolutely or relatively. Egolessness of dharmas, on the other hand, is realizing that they don't exist in the absolute but appear in the relative. But again, the appearance doesn't mean it's intrinsic, without causes and conditions, permanent, or singular. We relate to everything in that way, like this table. I relate to this table as one table. I do not relate to this table as something made up of trillions of particles, right? Also, yesterday's table and today's table I see this as one table. I relate to this as permanent. When I relate to this table, I don't really think of the causes and conditions that make this table come together. I relate to this table as a solid thing existing by itself.

We relate to the phenomenal world in this way. In both cases, it's mind's delusion. Whether we think that self exists as singular, permanent, intrinsic, and therefore solid, or that the phenomenal world is singular, permanent, intrinsic, and solid—both are projections of the ignorant, deluded mind. In the case of the self, it doesn't even exist in the relative world, but the phenomenon does appear. Appearance is all illusory—there is nothing substantial to it. This understanding brings us to realization. Mind does not perceive on the absolute level. Even on the relative level it does not recognize that the appearance of the *skandhas* are numerous, impermanent, and dependent upon causes and conditions.

The question comes to mind, who is the doer and who experiences the deeds? The answer to both is the mind. Once again, our mind doesn't correctly experience the doer and the deed. If the doer is the experiencer of the deed, and the doer has not changed, both cause and effect would be one. The doer becomes permanent, which cannot be a doer. What actually happens here is that the continuum of the doer experiences the deed. The experiencer is the continuum of the doer, not the doer itself. The doer itself has ceased. It is like an apple seed that produces a shoot. The moment the shoot has been produced, the apple seed has ceased to exist. The shoot is the continuum of that apple seed. Likewise the big apple tree that comes later is the continuum of the seed and the shoot. Relatively speaking, it's all one continuum.

There's no self that experiences; there's only the mind that experiences, and the mind is not permanent—it's the continuum that experiences. That's how karma works. Karma works based on things being impermanent. If something is permanent, karma cannot work. From that point of view we realize that all this relative experience of karma exists in illusion. In reality, when we realize emptiness, there is nothing as a doer or deed or the result being experienced. Only having completely made a home in the absolute do we transcend the relative experience. Until that point has come, we always have to experience in the relative, because we are absorbed in the relative world. In that way, even though karma doesn't exist in the absolute sense, we are still subject to it as long as we have not completely made a home in the absolute, completely realized the absolute truth.

When you have completely made a home in absolute truth, you have no reason to do anything negative. Negative action is done solely because of ignorant grasping to the self. Our confusion produces the afflicting emotions. Once free of this confusion, doing harm to others ceases. There's no reason to do anything negative. You do engage in the positive, but you don't cling to the positive having a reality or a substantial nature in any way. You do it as a means to accumulate merit, so that you can actually further your realization of emptiness and purify your obscurations.

The ultimate point here is that this wisdom of selflessness or egolessness—this wisdom of dharmas and the individual self—brings us to overcome our ignorance, confusions, delusions, afflicting emotions, negative karma, and what the negative karma produces, namely samsara. That realization is the most crucial thing on the path to enlightenment. That realization doesn't come from the practice of generosity, from the practice of discipline, or from the practice of patience. It doesn't come from diligently engaging in any of these practices, nor from the meditation of simply calming our mind. That realization only comes from the practice of wisdom. That wisdom does not come from the hearing wisdom or the contemplative wisdom. It only comes from an awakening deep within our own mind—being able to see the truth based on what we have heard and contemplated.

Once more, the awakened state of mind is absolute *bodhichitta*. The rest of it is relative *bodhichitta* practice, which involves accumulating merit through the practices of generosity, discipline, patience, diligence, and meditation, or by cultivating the hearing and contemplative wisdoms. These all set the condition for the practitioner to gain absolute realization. There's sort of a conditioning that needs to take place for you to get to that point. If these are not practiced, you won't have the proper conditions for the realization of absolute truth to dawn. Imagine having a realization of that absolute truth while you're constantly trying to secure the self and are so attached to possessions, or to merit, or to the body. How could you realize absolute *bodhichitta*? You couldn't. Engaging in generosity practice—letting go of some of that securing and protecting the self through your body or possessions—brings you further along to that realization. Once you have lost some of that very habitual attachment to securing the self with your possessions and merit, first in the mind, then slowly in actuality by giving it away, being inspired to do this more because of how far it actually moves you from suffering and the cause of suffering. Then you are automatically engaged and much further along the path.

That itself is merit. Merit is the effect that delivers you, which brings you along. When you constantly engage in negative actions due to afflicting emotions and self-grasping, how can you have any actual realization of absolute truth?

The discipline principle is to refrain from harming another as best you can and then to increase that effort, so that eventually you get to the point of not harming anyone in any way. This discipline frees you from old habits and brings you along the path, setting the conditions for you to realize the absolute truth. On top of it, practicing virtue, by observing vows and precepts, actually increases your positive energy, your positive inner strength, and is a remedy to negative habitual patterns, afflicting emotions, self-grasping, and ignorant mind. Following the vows and precepts brings you along to realization.

Trying to benefit others is the main part of the bodhisattva's discipline, and it brings you along to the realization of absolute truth. If you get angry all the time, that's because of holding on to the self—seeing others as a threat and yourself as being threatened. You are using your anger as protection. It's going to be very difficult to realize the absolute truth if you are constantly behaving like that. Practicing patience in ways that are suggested brings you further along to the realization of the absolute truth.

Diligently practicing generosity, patience, and discipline is the practice of the relative. Part of meditation is the relative, while part of meditation is the absolute. Diligence can be a support for the relative as well as a support for absolute practice. However, if your mind is constantly distracted and untamed, you cannot have realization of the absolute truth. Calm your mind by using the practices of loving-kindness, compassion, sympathetic joy, or equanimity as the focal point. Meditating on these, or trying to calm one's mind, is called *samten* practice.

It's all a preparation for the realization of absolute truth. My point is that generosity, discipline, patience, diligence, and meditation all bring you closer and closer to realization of the absolute. These practices train your mind, helping it to not be consumed by old habits and afflicting emotions. They help you to not grasp onto the self so violently from the ignorant habit that has been formed.

Ultimately, although you practice all of these, you will not obtain nirvana without wisdom. You will have better karma and better future rebirths in samsara, but if there is no awakening from ignorance itself, you are not going to obtain nirvana. These are, however, the causes and circumstances that condition you to have wisdom. The wisdom of the realization of the absolute truth that is universal enlightened mind liberates you from all ignorance and delusion and frees you from circling in samsara.

Wisdom is the most important *paramita*. The reason why we move sequentially from generosity to discipline, discipline to patience, patience to diligence, diligence to meditation, is that it is a natural progression of the path. For instance, if you are strongly attached to this life, this body, these possessions, it's very difficult to practice discipline. You are going to be hindered by attachments. Generosity practice prepares you to have better discipline by loosening these attachments. It's actually easier to do than discipline because it has more to do with outer things.

When you have discipline, you are more prepared to have patience. Patience is tolerance, not out of weakness but out of strength. There is a difference between tolerance out of weakness and tolerance out of strength. Tolerance that comes from strength has an overview and an understanding of a situation, as well as a farsightedness. It is the opposite of giving in to weakness.

When you have patience, you are more prepared to be diligent in the practice of the spiritual path. Diligence that comes from delight and joy is genuine diligence, while diligence that is driven by ambition and ego is not necessarily considered diligence. From this point of view it must be out of delight and joy. This comes from actually knowing the whole path and gaining inspiration from that. You have a sense of what you are getting into and what can result as a benefit for your future well-being. The traditional image is that of a swan swimming in a lake. It's a delightful action for a swan to swim in a lake.

With diligence, you can develop deeper meditation. Meditation here means a stable mind, an unmoving mind that is steadied through concentration. The mind here is not so involved in sensory objects. With this deeper meditation, you can experience the dawn of the realization of absolute truth. The final *paramita* is *sherab,* known as the most excellent knowledge, because this knowledge can bring us to the other shore of samsara.

The six *paramitas* are taught in this particular order because it's easier for us to enter the path that way. The first *paramita* becomes a stepping-stone for doing well in the second—each prepares us to master the next. Without doing well in the first one, it becomes almost impossible to do the second. That's why the *paramitas* are ordered in this way.

The dawn of enlightenment, which we wish not only for ourselves but also for the benefit of others, is really the wisdom that actually sees the truth as it is—nothing more, nothing less. Truth itself is enlightenment. Truth realized is the state of nirvana. There's no need for anything other than that to overcome the experiences and delusions of samsara. There's nothing greater than the truth itself. That truth is known as *prajñaparamita,* the mother *paramita.* Realization of that truth, Mother Prajñaparamita, gives birth to all buddhas, bodhisattvas, *pratyekabuddhas,* and *shravakas.*

If that truth were not the natural nirvana and the realization of it the perfect enlightenment, then enlightenment would be something that you created. Something that you created would not be suitable for others. The Buddha realized the truth. Since it is the truth itself, it is the natural nirvana. The realization of that is the perfect enlightenment. The awareness of natural nirvana, enlightenment, is within the reach of all beings, since all beings have that truth as their disposition, as their heritage.

Now, when you intend to become enlightened for the benefit of all beings, you must realize that you are not in some kind of cult or on an ego trip. You are not in a science fiction pursuit. If that were the case, it would not be of benefit to many people. Even if you got to wherever you wanted to go, it would be useless—most probably not only for you, but for others as well. But the enlightened human being is not a science fiction fantasy or the result of a cult. The path to enlightenment is the pursuit of the truth, the ultimate truth that actually exists as truth for all. If you realize the truth, it can overcome all that you and others suffer within samsara. That realization can actually enable you to benefit many others.

All beings suffer. Realizing the natural truth and becoming enlightened enables you to share that insight, to show them the path and guide them to overcome their suffering. This is a tremendous benefit to many, to whomever is ready.

Meanwhile, even on the path, we need generosity, discipline, patience, diligence, meditation, and wisdom. Everyone suffers from stinginess, from wrongdoing, lack of virtue, impatience, aggression, laziness, distraction, and ignorance. The six *paramitas* of generosity, discipline, patience, diligence, meditation, and wisdom are needed to combat these frames of mind. If somebody wants to be enlightened, all six *paramitas* are necessary. From this very practical point of view, the Buddhist teachings and the path are not so much a religion as a science.

Diligence is what makes the difference between a great practitioner, a medium practitioner, and an insignificant practitioner.

Your degree of diligence depends on how inspired you are. Your inspiration depends upon how you motivate yourself by using your thoughts and feelings. You can arouse inspiration through your own sense of reasoning, by looking for profit or benefit. The internal dialogue you should have is something like this: "If there is such profit and benefit to be harvested, why don't I harvest them? What is the loss and danger that I might or might not encounter? Why don't I secure this great profit and benefit that will secure me life after life in bliss and happiness?"

A lot of people don't like to have internal dialogues because they prefer to act impulsively. Internal dialogue and reasoning make them tired [*Laughs*]. In this case, however, you must have an internal dialogue. You can't act impulsively. If you do, you are simply acting out of habit—out of afflicting emotions, confusion, and the ego. Internal dialogue can purify your ignorance and confusion, your doubts and gullible state of mind. Though these negative thought patterns may not be actively manifesting, they hinder you by creating obstacles to motivation and inspiration. When you purify these through internal dialogue, those obstacles are gone. However, it takes a certain amount of effort to inspire yourself through internal dialogue.

In general, thinking about problems, dangers, and potential loss can make you depressed. Why think about something that makes you feel depressed? I suppose that's why many don't like to have internal dialogues. In this case, however, it's not going to make you depressed, because the aim here is to inspire and motivate yourself. If you truly know in an emotional sense all the risks, the dangers, the profits, and the benefits involved, then the situation becomes a little more real than a game you're playing. When you play a game of Monopoly, you know it's a game and are not so emotionally invested. You don't care much if you lose or win. But if it's a real sort of game, like the stock market, you are emotionally invested. This can actually motivate you. Sometimes having your emotions involved is a very great way to motivate and inspire yourself. When you feel things are directly related to your life, it can make you more inspired and motivated. That's why Shantideva uses this method a lot in his book.

As he writes in the beginning of the text, "I'm not trying to teach anybody. I'm trying to practice myself. And in order to make progress myself, I am going to reveal what I've tried to practice." He talks about the pains and sufferings of hell, and how tragic it would be if, knowing how painful they are, we still enter them. We have the chance to avoid the hells, yet we don't do what we need to do in order to avoid them. Most of *The Way of the Bodhisattva* is Shantideva's own internal dialogue. Many Western people don't like to motivate themselves in this way, but it's a very effective method.

Being emotionally involved is a great way to become motivated and inspired. Inspire yourself to have internal dialogue. To have an internal dialogue, you have to have reasoning. In order for the reasoning to be really personal, you need to acknowledge your own personal and emotional investment. Eventually, as you go further and become more realized, you don't need to work with emotional investment, because you have secured your position. You have gotten a degree of freedom already, so you don't have to worry so much. In the beginning, however, it's a very effective method to think of the loss, the danger, and the suffering that you might have to endure versus the profit, the benefit, the happiness, and the bliss that you could experience.

We are really like spoiled children, absolutely unappreciative of what's good for us. For a kid who's spoiled rotten, some discipline is important. Knowing that we are spoiled, that our heart and behavior are rotten, we need strict discipline with a certain fear. Now, if a child has no potential at all, it's very difficult, of course. But most of the time, there is potential—it's just that we can't help the way we behave sometimes. To cure these patterns, we need to know the dangers and have some degree of fear of them.

When others try to instill this fear, it doesn't work—you go the opposite way. There's this dynamic between yourself and others. When you yourself do something, fully knowing why you are doing it and what the objective is, then you see a point. Otherwise, why do it? Doing it yourself really works, especially for a person like me. I know that it doesn't work from the outside, but from the inside it really works. I could be very lazy and simply indulge in the laziness. I actually try to wake myself up from that laziness by thinking about impermanence and death, or the suffering that awaits me in the lower realms. That can really motivate me [*Snaps fingers*]. I feel really glad that I actually am able to think about impermanence and the suffering of the lower realms, because it motivates me. But if somebody were to say to me, "You're going to die and be reborn in the lower realms," I might not be inspired. I might actually put one pillow on top of another over my head and go to sleep! So you see, an internal dialogue can be much more effective than someone speaking at you from the outside.

A Can-Do Attitude

SHANTIDEVA'S CHAPTER ON DILIGENCE is interesting because usually we try not to be arrogant, but here we're encouraged to be a little arrogant, a little cocky. I think it works because people with a can-do attitude often accomplish things. Here, I suppose Shantideva is encouraging us to be choleric personality types. Choleric[3] people are good at organizing and carrying things out. Laid-back people who don't do much are called phlegmatic. "Can do, why not, of course, sure, it's easy" personalities are positive thinkers. They generally have a lot of energy to do things, and they get them done.

Sometimes they are a little bit too much. Too much self-confidence can appear as arrogance and pride. They seem like they want to take over and rule, and don't think about whether others want to follow or not. Maybe others actually want to do the same thing, but they don't want to be led by the nose or told what to do. This gets the choleric personality type in trouble—not being sensitive enough to others, even though they are just taking the lead because something needs to get done for the good of the community or the situation, not necessarily for their own personal benefit. But people like myself who are phlegmatic don't like to be pushed around. If there are quite a few phlegmatics in the group, at some point friction will start. The positive side, though, is that a can-do mentality does not hesitate or feel tired, and it gets results.

In this case I don't think one is going to get into trouble, because the can-do attitude Shantideva is talking about is not applied to outer things. It's about internal accomplishment, overcoming one's own obscurations, habitual patterns, self-importance, and ignorance. It cannot go wrong. One applies this mentality within oneself, in order to practice, accumulate wisdom, abandon the negative emotions and self-clinging, and obtain realization of wisdom.

As a teacher, I know something about people who are afraid of their mind and their emotions—those who have a mind-set that says, "Oh, I can't. It's too hard. It's beyond me. I'm over-whelmed." Such individuals are undermined by their own men-tality. Before they even engage in practice to work with their mind, and particularly their self-importance, they are overcome. It's not so much a matter of low self-esteem; rather, it's not want-ing to put in the effort. Some people do not want to put in the effort because they've already decided it's better to fail. That's a very difficult situation, because on the one hand, students come to become healthy and for the support from the teacher. On the other hand, it's almost like there's the expectation that the teacher can do the work for them. If they have to work on their own, they would rather sink than swim. This kind of dynamic perhaps comes from having somebody else do a lot of things for them as a child, so that they never had to do things for themselves. Or even if they had to do something themselves, they had a great deal of support, encouragement, and help from outside.

With this type of person, work is more important for others than themselves. It's like a child eating: Sometimes it's more for the mother than for the kid. Children sometimes feel that they are eating for their parents. That pattern still continues. It's not conscious, but it's still there. That can become very difficult; because there's no way that someone can do this work for you. You have to do it yourself. This fact can become very mentally painful. Until this is surmounted, the work will not get done and you will be stuck. Even if you have all the capacities, the means, the actual knowledge, and the strength, there is a blind spot that makes it so you cannot get away from being like a child. It's feeling like you are obligated to someone else. Do not think you owe anybody. Do what needs to be done for yourself, and rise above the neurosis. It takes a great deal of merit for one to have light shine on this blind spot. In *lojong,* mind training we have a saying: "Don't think you owe anyone if you are doing practice." A starving person eats for his own hunger, not for his mother's sake.

There is also the frame of mind that wants to justify your existence through thinking that your practice is done for many others. There can be attachment to the self-importance of doing it for the benefit of others, so that your own existence is justified as something significant. That kind of attachment makes the mind weak and impoverished. It's like cooking: If you make a nice dinner for yourself, you don't feel like somebody else owes you anything. You are just making a nice dinner for yourself. But if you make a nice dinner for someone else, there can be the danger of thinking, "Oh, this person owes me something." The bodhisattva's way of benefiting for others should be more like you making a nice dinner for yourself. That is your happiness. That is the way that you actually experience your own fulfillment.

It's very difficult for the teacher when the student is stuck there. It's hard to know what to do—be harsh and pop somebody out of that? Often that doesn't work. People get hurt. These are not children, after all. Maybe you could actually discipline your children and be a little bit sharp, but these are adults. When people get hurt, they can turn in many directions that are not going to be helpful. On the other hand, you can't wait forever for people to get over their neurosis. The clock is ticking. You have to do some prayers and maybe perhaps encourage them to do meritorious deeds so that they can be free of this internal dynamic. The person needs to become aware that, "I am hungry, and the food to quell that hunger is right in front of me." They need the mindset that, "By eating this food, I'll fill my belly, nourish my body, and get over being fatigued. Then I can be strong and move on in life." It is important to realize that Dharma practice and benefiting beings is for the freedom, realization, and enlightenment of our mind. We can take teachings, train in them, and have the practice truly overcome the obscurations. We can actually attain realization and enlightenment.

Develop this deep sense of determination and courage, this can-do mentality and self-confidence. It will bring you far along the path. If you don't have it, work more to get it. The can-do types get many more results in Dharma practice, because there's no conflict going on in their mind. People with self-doubts and internal conflicts use more energy getting things done. With a lack of self-confidence, more work just piles on you. So, to have this can-do mentality and "why not, of course, sure, very well" attitude is mind training. That's what is explained here.

In the West, people wait to be inspired instead of inspiring themselves. A lot of the time they're waiting for feelings—fishing for feelings, instead of seeing that feelings are compounded things that can be cultivated due to causes and conditions. People here think that if the feeling of inspiration is cultivated, then maybe it's not so genuine. If it "comes," it's genuine. But that's not true. Nothing comes without causes and conditions.

There is not enough contemplation wisdom. People go to teachings as if they were going to listen to a symphony. When you go to hear music, you just sit back, relax, and the music plays. However the music moves your mind is how it is. Going to a Dharma lecture, you hear the teachings. The hearing wisdom involves whatever resonates in your mind, touches you, makes sense, and enlightens your mind. If you don't follow up on that with contemplative wisdom, contemplative effort, it stops right there. The problem of being unable to inspire yourself actually comes from being unable to successfully contemplate the teachings. You need to know how to contemplate creatively. You can mix the various teachings you've received to properly contemplate a subject. If you are lacking incentive, contemplate impermanence and get motivated. Or, if you do not have enough renunciation, contemplate the sufferings of samsara. If you lack faith, contemplate the reasons to have faith and the qualities of the Buddha, the Dharma, and the *Sangha*. Reflect on how the Dharma works for the benefit of beings as well as your own personal achievement.

All of those are relative things. You have to learn how to apply contemplative mind to move forward in practice. If you just want to use your mind without the hearing wisdom, you're like a blind person trying to hit somebody with a stick. It's almost impossible. But with hearing wisdom, you have a ground for contemplative wisdom. Using your contemplative mind to shape, direct, guide, and cultivate your mind in the way you want to is big fun. Most of the time you are not in charge—neurosis is in charge. With contemplative wisdom, however, you are in charge.

Of course, there are times when you are not motivated. For instance, you don't want to get up in the early morning and get in your car when it's very cold, snowy, and dark. You would rather sleep. But it's a Monday, it's a workday, and you have to get to work. If you don't get to work, there will be consequences. Even though you have the wish to sleep for another five minutes, you don't. You get up, leave the house, scrape the windshield, heat the car, and go to work. When you are motivated because you know the reasons to do something and the consequences of not doing it, then things get done. Sometimes there are more serious things that you don't want to do, like having an operation. Who wants to undergo an operation? Who wants to be cut open? Who wants to have their heart pumped by a machine? Who wants all of these drastic things done to oneself? Knowing the reasons for doing it and the consequences of not doing it motivates you. These are the facts and figures laid out on the table by life. You have to make a choice. You try to make the best choice to live and survive, to keep this life going. There are many things in life that no one feels inspired to do, but you do them anyway.

Similarly, when you feel stuck in the practice of Dharma, you have to find your way out. Cultivate the hearing wisdom and use your contemplative mind to bring you out of that stuck place. In doing so, you become an independent practitioner, able to walk on your own two feet. In conventional situations, you train in one profession. If you were trained as a lawyer, you would never know anything about medicine—you'd have to seek the advice of a doctor if you fell sick. But in the Dharma it's not like that. When you train in the Dharma, you are trying to know all aspects of your mind—your thoughts, your emotions, and the remedies for those neuroses. You learn all aspects of the path and what is necessary on that path.

To know about the law is a tremendous amount of work. Just getting into law school is difficult. The cost of getting a law degree can be more than a hundred thousand dollars. But the Dharma is not like that. It takes one book like this, the *Bodhicharyavatara,* as an example. Study it over and over and learn it. Cultivate the hearing wisdom, next contemplate and, finally, train in meditation. This alone will set you completely on your two feet. When you read any profound text, gain an understanding of what is being said. Learn how to study it, contemplate it, and meditate on it to the fullest extent. If you truly study one text, most likely it is going to be much easier to study the next text, and the next. After a couple of texts all these treasures of the Buddha's teachings, these works by great teachers, will be at your disposal. You can really have a feast of teachings as a resource to apply to your mind. There's no fee for it, when you are able to read, understand, and apply. Initially it's very important to get some hearing wisdom from the teacher, but often after that most of the studies are done by yourself. All teachings will be medicine for your mind: medicine for the afflicting emotions, obscurations, the ego, and all of its harmful habitual patterns. The remedies are the same in each case: egolessness of the self, egolessness of the dharmas, generating the *bodhichitta* of aspiration, and practicing the *bodhichitta* of engagement.

My point here is that learning how to use your mind is both the greatest challenge and the greatest reward. Learning how to use your mind to its fullest potential is the work of Dharma. The reward is the realization of truth itself. The reason why it's challenging is not because you lack intelligence. Western people are very intelligent and study all their lives. Basically, from the age of three onwards, they are going to school. Westerners have the disposition and training to study, as well as the intelligence to do so. For someone who's been a farmer or a butcher all his life and never actually read a book, it would be different. He would be good at butchering or farming, but wouldn't have the disposition for literature.

The challenge in this case is that with this approach you may always need a manual or instructions to guide you from the outside, rather than being able to follow your inner knowing. Sometimes this can make you even worse than an illiterate person fresh out of Tibet. For example, when a new machine comes and there is no manual, Western people get very puzzled and don't know what to do. I once saw some monks who came from Tibet trying to assemble a machine without a manual. They took the thing out, looked at it from all sides, used their minds, and put it together. This kind of training in figuring it out on your own, using your own resources—there's not so much emphasis on that in the West. Things are always being made so easy, with manuals and texts, everything comes with an explanation. Westerners get dependent on that, and it makes for difficulties. I was very surprised by this.

Once I was in Bir, in India, when a gadget came to our monastery. There was a monk from Tibet and a few Western students. There were no instructions for the thing. The Western students said, "There are no instructions; it's nearly hopeless. Just leave it there." The monk played with it and figured out how to assemble it and make it work. What I'm trying to say through this example is that it can be a challenge for Western people to use their own mind without manuals and transcripts, to skillfully influence their mind in the right direction.

The challenge is to use our own mind to reach the deepest aspects of our intelligence. There is no chance of that happening without the hearing wisdom. We owe so much to the buddhas, to the great teachers who left behind all these teachings. The Buddha went through so much trouble to cultivate just one word of wisdom for the benefit of others. It's not for novelty that the teachers wrote the various texts. They wrote them for future generations.

In the beginning, you need the hearing wisdom. Once you are on your own two feet, you will be able to run in the field of Dharma. To get to that point, do a lot of reading and apply it to your experience, bringing your profound intelligence to the surface. Then you will be able to transform your mind and assimilate the Dharma. Until you integrate the Dharma in your being, it remains as mere theory.

The process of reading can be almost like dancing on a book. You get glimpses of what's being said, but it's not yet internalized—you close the book and you go blank. There's not really any understanding of how to apply what's written in the book in daily life. However, when you know how to relate personally to what you read in the book and you can identify your internal understanding according to what you read, using it to illuminate your own experience, that is when your mind and the Dharma have been integrated. You're no longer dancing on the surface of the book.

You must have this feeling of self-confidence and a can-do mentality. Don't focus so much on the hindrances, but rather on what needs to be done. Then get it done. Recently a blind man climbed Mount Everest. Achievement like this comes from a certain state of mind. People who have more hindrances can still do their work if they have a can-do mentality. People with the mind-set of "I can't do it" never get anything done, even if they have fewer hindrances. Here Shantideva is encouraging us to have the can-do mentality, as well as the "why not" mentality.

To be able to change your mind is really much more profitable, more beneficial, than changing your career. I really am quite confident that if people have the mentality of "I can practice" rather than "I can't practice," "I can actually overcome my neurosis" versus "I am overwhelmed by my neurosis," then they will be successful in Dharma practice. It's a matter of having the mind-set of "easy" rather than "hard." Of course, you will have to work a little bit, but that will be implementing the "easy" mentality instead of, "Oh, I will have to work very hard, and it will be very difficult."

By actually going ahead and doing it, your practice will change within a month—even within a week. It can change your way of relating to your practice and your way of relating with your mind in practice. I've seen this repeatedly with people in retreat. Some people work very hard but with a feeling of how hard it is to be in retreat, how difficult it is to work with their mind, how horrific it is to see their mind. It just goes on and on and on. They work very hard, practicing twelve hours a day, but make very little progress. For others it may be hard in the beginning, but, with the can-do mentality, they very quickly take to practice and start to transform their minds, which become much more agile and integrated with the practice.

Others, who are not bodhisattvas, who are in samsara in the conventional world, are not going to be able to do much to benefit you, because they are on the wrong track. If the root is poison, the trunk and the branch and the leaf and the fruit will all be poison. Even though sentient beings desire happiness and long for freedom from suffering, trying to achieve that by focusing on the self is the wrong track. The outcome will be afflicting emotions, negative karma, and samsara's delusion.

Conversely, the bodhisattva has decided to focus on the happiness and freedom of all. That is the root of a tree that will grow the fruits of loving-kindness, compassion, sympathetic joy, equanimity, generosity, discipline, patience, diligence, meditation, and wisdom. Since all beings long for freedom from suffering, there is no reason to focus on the self, which brings only suffering. Why not focus on all beings? That is the beginning of altruism. That is the seed that gives birth to *bodhichitta*, which is what actually brings happiness to others and happiness to oneself. It is the right track.

A bodhisattva on the right track has the resources of wisdom and skillful means. When you're on the right track, why not work hard? Everyone knows that if their heart becomes infused with loving-kindness, compassion, sympathetic joy, and equanimity, and their mind filled with generosity, discipline, patience, meditation, and wisdom, it's certain that they're going to be much happier. There's no doubt about that. Clinging to self-importance, the afflicting emotions, and negative habitual patterns will not make you happy. That's no mystery. That aspect has to be brought to the forefront of your awareness. When you know something for sure, you have clarity, and you have to act on that. Acting upon that clarity, you have many resources. All the wisdom and skillful means that the buddhas and bodhisattvas have applied are at your disposal. You will be successful: Have confidence in this. If you are one hundred percent guaranteed to make a profit, you have to work, don't you? Basically, from your own innate, intuitive intelligence, know what has and has not worked. Place your confidence in what has worked for the buddhas and bodhisattvas, not in what has not worked for sentient beings. This kind of self-confidence inspires you.

If you don't have some form of self-confidence and conviction and you give in to low self-esteem and this "can't-do" mind, you'll be threatened by all your little neuroses and overwhelmed by your weaknesses. But simply giving up will not bring benefit, either in this life or the next. With such a mind there is not going to be a possibility of liberation. From within, develop a sense of self-confidence and pride that you will be able to overcome your neuroses. If you are victorious over neuroses, both enlightenment and the benefit of others are assured. Otherwise, having the wish to benefit others but being unable to overcome your own neuroses is nothing more than a bluff. We need Buddha's fearlessness, that kind of confidence.

Next, practice very joyfully, like a child at play. However long children play, they never tire of it. They want to have fun continuously until they are completely exhausted and fall asleep. The moment they wake up they want to play again. Children have a lot of fun doing it. We must actually practice the *paramitas* like that. Something that is so profound and deep greatly frees and supports our mind, both now and in the future. Of course we must take a deep delight in practicing that. Most of the time conventional happiness is like honey on a razor blade. We flash the credit card—easy. When the bill comes—big headache. But here, the joy is continuous. It's like a very hot elephant coming to a lake. There is absolutely no hesitation for the elephant to jump in there and swim. Like Labrador retrievers when they see a river or a swan in a lake—there's no hesitation to go in. In this way, when there is a practice to do, show no hesitation. This is all in relation to enjoying what we are doing.

Then when illness, tiredness, or other obstacles challenge you, leave the meditation session so that you can return it and not get jaded. People have a hard time settling into meditation. They exert a lot of effort trying to settle; they struggle and struggle. Finally their energy gets settled, and their mind becomes calm. Then they meditate too long, burn out, and don't return to the cushion for a whole year. Because they've practiced too long, they are not inspired to do meditation the next time. This happens often. So practice, and when the time is over, stop. Come back to it; next time will be better. Doing short sessions, extending them to what is possible and not stretching beyond that, is very important.

Additionally, you need mindfulness. Just as you would not want to drop your weapon on a battlefield, don't drop your mindfulness. If you drop your weapon, you might be killed the next minute. If you drop your mindfulness, you might be hit hard by your neurosis. Thinking of the suffering that neurosis causes in this life and the next, always hold on to mindfulness. Always apply mindfulness.

It's important to apply mindfulness when it's needed, and then to relax once it's applied. Be relaxed as well as diligent. It's like driving. You apply your mindfulness to not go over into the next lane, especially on a two-lane highway, right? If you want to go into the next lane, you check your side mirror; you check your rearview mirror, even the blind spot. Then you turn on the blinker and go. All of this is mindfulness. Otherwise you could cause an accident.

Always apply your mindfulness in this way, quickly and reflexively. If a man is very easily scared and a snake drops into his lap, there's going to be an automatic reaction. Or if somebody is very aware of her looks and her hair catches on fire, she will immediately put out the fire. When any small neurosis comes, respond like that—very quickly and immediately. If some little feeling of resentment is burning inside, attend to it and overcome it with the practice of loving-kindness or compassion or forgiveness, whatever is necessary.

When one of your neuroses hits you and you can't avoid it, spend a lot of time analyzing it: Ask yourself, "How did it come? Why did it come? What was the cause? How did it actually all happen? Where did I fall short? What was my weakness?" Focus on changing yourself so that next time you can avoid repeating that same mistake. Engender mindfulness and critical intelligence. Mindfulness is like when you're walking on the edge of a cliff, aware of the big drop. Critical intelligence involves knowing what to do and how to apply yourself. The combinations of mindfulness, critical intelligence, a joyful attitude, inspiration, and self-confidence will make your body, speech, and mind agile like the wind. Wherever you choose to direct your mind, it can easily go there, just like a piece of cotton carried by the breeze. Think about the benefits and gain, be inspired, and it will be quite easy to practice.

Anything we love doing is easy to do. This is what brings all the great practitioners to become great masters. If you look at Dilgo Khyentse Rinpoche or Tulku Urgyen Rinpoche or any of the great masters, practice is effortless for them—a very natural thing. For them to apply themselves to the practice of Dharma or to do anything to benefit others is utterly unforced. There's so much joy, so much deep appreciation and delight in doing it.

This is the way, then, we must practice diligence. If you have any questions, go ahead.

Student: When you talk about attachment and fear, would you talk a little bit more about what it is we are afraid of?

Rinpoche: We are afraid of losing this self, hurting this self—basically, of having this self be hurt. A lot of the time we fear having ourselves experience pain. As I said, though, there is no self in the absolute sense, and not even in the relative sense. Our fear is actually the mind's own apprehension of suffering. Mind suffers because of its belief in the self. The self is attached to whatever it is attached to. Relaxing the belief in the self's true existence, experiencing its empty nature, seeing relative phenomenon as illusory, these all help mind not be so attached to the self, or to anything else.

That doesn't mean that if somebody does something to hurt you, you won't suffer. Let's say someone calls you a bad name or gets angry with you. Even though you have already realized there's no real self and that all experiences of mind are illusory, the suffering comes from the residue of having believed in the self, which is not yet completely cleansed. Still, you won't suffer as much as before, especially if you can actually be aware of the selflessness of the ego or of the mind. At that point you are under the power of habit rather than of clarity. Over time, as the mind becomes free of that habit or the residue of old habits, you are not going to suffer at all.

I think *lojong*—mind training practice in post-meditation—is very helpful during this in-between time. This is when the practitioner has some conceptual glimpse of the egolessness of the mind and some realization that the self doesn't exist in the relative sense, but that the mind does exist in the relative as an illusory appearance. *Lojong* gives you something to do. Since you are not able to immediately enter into the *samadhi* of emptiness when that habit kicks in, you have to respond to what is happening inside your mind. First, be with that raw pain, without necessarily trying to do anything. Gain some strength. Once you gain some internal strength to be with the pain, you can think, "Oh, that person has done what they did out of confusion. I should feel sorry for the person, who must be enduring so much suffering. May that person be free from such suffering and such anger." This can actually help. Or you could think, "Oh you know, such a thing could be said to another person and they would not be offended. Since I am offended, it clearly proves that it's my self-importance. Actually this is good for me, this will reduce my self-importance." Behave in that way instead of being upset. Actually appreciate it. This can also overcome the feeling of hurt.

Lojong is a relative practice working with thoughts and emotions, manipulating them in a positive direction. It is something that we can easily do. The results we can expect are very simple as well. Now, as we progress in meditation practice, become stable and able to rest in the nature much more consistently without any distractions, the *lojong* would most probably not be so much of a necessity.

I think the ideal way to practice is to put *lojong* and Dzogchen practice hand in hand. Do a lot of *lojong* practice during post-meditation, since you are more frequently in that state. It seems that you will still find old habitual reactions, even though you meditate a lot, lot, lot. That's why even though you may practice Dzogchen, always having some *lojong* practice to assist the Dzogchen practice is very important. Otherwise, there still seems to be some danger of reacting in the old ways.

Meditation

The Way of the Bodhisattva's chapter on meditation is one of the most important chapters in the whole text. It gives clear guidance on how to meditate on *bodhichitta* and all the reasons for meditating in this way. This is the main practice of relative *bodhichitta*. Absolute *bodhichitta*, of course, is explained in the wisdom chapter. Relative *bodhichitta*, as mentioned earlier, is the practice of equalizing oneself and others and of exchanging oneself for others. This chapter begins with teachings on abandoning distractions and then discusses meditation, *samten* on *bodhichitta*. This meditation involves equalizing and subsequently exchanging others and oneself. Through it, one learns how to see others and oneself as equal, how to exchange oneself for others, and the reasons for and wisdom of doing so. Just as the patience chapter is the antidote for aggression, this chapter is the antidote for attachment or lust. The wisdom chapter is the antidote for ignorance. These are the three main antidotes for the three main poisons. The rest of the chapters are to assist these three remedies.

Working with our minds in accordance with the patience chapter, we can overcome the gross and subtle levels of aggression and our minds will become very peaceful. Working with desire and lust according to the meditation chapter, our minds will become deeply calm. Usually we are very reactive people;

here we are struggling not to be. There's still a ways to go to make mind, even though not reactive, deeply calm.

In speaking of this we come to *sepa*, which is craving brought on by lust. Whenever there is craving, mind is not calm. Our minds are somewhat like a dog seeing a big piece of meat right in front of its nose. That will not make the dog very calm and peaceful. Mind is not calm when lust manifests from craving. When that mind is remedied, then mind is freed from that particular craving and can be calm.

There are two ways to remedy craving: first, by realizing emptiness, and second, by actually trying to bring some sense to the craving. There are many teachings on the first remedy. With the second remedy here, you reason with your lust that is actively engaging the craving. Focus on the object and have some aversion. Aversion as taught here has more to do with how irony exists in your own mind. For example, you see something that is beautiful and attractive and you have a tremendous craving for it. From another perspective you can examine it in a way that reveals it to be dirty, gross, unappealing, and disgusting. Actually it is the same object you are seeing. The difference lies in how it presents itself to your mind. One minute you see how gross a piece of dog poop is: smelly and disgusting. However, if it is covered with chocolate and scented with vanilla and presented to you, it becomes appealing and attractive. A buddha, on the other hand, does not make judgments regarding clean and unclean, as these are merely concepts. Since buddhas don't have concepts, they don't cling to any ideas or have that problem.

When meditating in order to have a deeper insight of absolute truth, a calm mind is very important. Mind continuously engaged in deep lust that forms fixations is very difficult to calm even in a quiet place. However, for a beginner to engage in meditation, he or she first has to disengage from distractions. Without abandoning distractions, mind and body will not be calm. Often the biggest distractions are the relationships you have with others. If you really sit back and examine it closely, in many ways that's where your mind is disturbed the most. That's simply the nature of relationships. Contemplate what distracts you the most. Is it needing company, somebody to be cozy with, or somebody to love you, care for you, be sweet to you, and be affectionate to you? It doesn't seem like there is any problem with this. It seems like a very good thing to have all of these, like there's nothing wrong with wanting these, nothing wrong or problematic even with having it. But relationships aren't always cozy, comforting, sweet, kind, and affectionate. If you could program the company, maybe it might happen. But you can't program human beings.

The desire or longing we have is somewhat naïve. We think, "Oh, it doesn't hurt to have this in my life." We get hooked to those romantic ideas, and we crave incessantly. We are always somewhat disappointed if it is not in our life. Sometimes we blame the world for it not being there, or others for not being programmed the way we want them to be. We can also get very hard on ourselves. "What's wrong with me? Why don't I have the perfect mate or perfect lover, the perfect company or the perfect this or that?" Then we see ourselves as a tremendous problem and become overly self-critical. Nonetheless, we still cannot let go of the longing or get over these naïve and romantic ideas. In books it appears to work that way, but most probably in real life, the novelist's mind is much more complicated. Honestly, even in novels it doesn't always have a happy ending.

Think about your lust, either subtle or great, that affects your heart by not letting it be calm. By its very nature lust makes you dissatisfied. People get excited, sure. Drug addicts and alcoholics get excited when they see drugs or alcohol. But that doesn't mean drugs or alcohol are good for them. Lust always manifests in that way. Some things we have ruled out as being unhealthy. Others we have accepted as healthy, or not exactly healthy per se, but normal. It is accepted as normal to have craving. Nonetheless, when lust rises in your heart, the momentary experience of calm, contentment, and peace changes into the next instant—disquiet, discontent, and restlessness. All of a sudden, you have to figure out what to do with this. All sorts of crazy thoughts come, and the crazy thoughts have to make a plan. And the plan has to be executed. Things may or may not go according to plan: That's how hopes and fears come. The mind boils: That's how lust starts. Anything can be mistaken for pleasure. Masochists relate to pain as pleasure. That doesn't mean that pain is pleasure. Anything can be related to as pleasure. Not that I'm making judgments about masochists, but that's just an example.

Here we are taking a scientific attitude. A practitioner has to be very objective about how everything works. From there, we have to make an assessment of what's healthy for us and what's not healthy for us, what supports our well-being and what doesn't support it. From that point of view, we must get over our craving as much as possible. If we can do this, we are definitely going to be content, calm, and at peace. Passing thoughts of craving leave an imprint in the heart. It is helpful to recognize our craving and think about whether it is something we want or need, whether it is something that is good for us. Always examine whether this is a good, healthy need. It might be a good thing, or it might not be healthy. If something were not healthy, why would we need it? Even if it's good or healthy, maybe we don't actually need it. We should guide our mind to arrive at the point where we are much more content to not have something than to have it.

Overcoming craving, clearing its residue from your heart, is very helpful. You can clear many cravings that otherwise pass through your mind and inevitably leave imprints in your heart— so much so that your heart becomes crowded with the imprints of many, many, many cravings. This leads to so much dissatisfaction and feelings of unhappiness. Of the ten negative actions, coveting is considered a major one by the Buddha because it creates so much suffering. If you want to find a calm, content, peaceful mind, it's helpful to rise above craving. Otherwise, mind begins to boil and work very actively from the subtle, small lust that springs up in the heart. Maybe it bursts forth as, "Oh, wonderful, go to Iraq and conquer Saddam Hussein, and turn all of Iraq around to be a democratic country. How great to make Iraq an example in the Middle East!" But there are problems in carrying through with such things.

Student: It's a can-do attitude.

Rinpoche: [*Laughs*] This kind of can-do attitude is guided by the wrong wisdom. Initially it probably came up in the mind as some kind of excitement. But look how that work turned out. It's obvious what's happening here. Things are just not that simple. It's always like that. We get enthused and romantic about something, and the circumstances don't really cooperate. When things are not going according to plan, then we work on it. When mind works on it, it gets stronger and stronger and stronger. It becomes ambitious. Mind works out of hopes and fears. It becomes a challenge to the ego. "Do this, do that, get this done, get that done."

This can become our whole life's mission, with years spent on it. When something first arises, it's easy to remedy through recognizing it. Later, when we have made it into a mission and have been working for it obsessively, it is harder to overcome.

Lust initially arises as a joy, as bliss. It is perceived as a fulfillment. But is it really going to be fulfilling, joyful, and blissful? That has not been thought through. There is always that naïveté in ordinary beings' minds. Nothing in samsara ever turns into true bliss, real happiness, and fulfillment. Due to the *alaya*,[4] the seed of karma germinates. All the conditions grab that seed, and it turns into a whole life's work.

We spend all of our time moving from one thing to the next like that. That's why we are mentally, emotionally, and physically fatigued, in the sense of being overworked. To rejuvenate from exhaustion, we must rest in the true natural state of mind. That's the only way to truly restore our energy. Even if we are trying to rest, it just doesn't work in samsara. If we want to rest on a Hawaiian beach, it turns into a big mission. We go to Hawaii, and when we get there it's cloudy [*Laughs*]. The only true rest is when we can rest in the natural state of mind. We cannot rest in regular samsaric mind any more than we can swim in turbulent water. Similarly, we cannot truly rest if we are unable to overcome lust and craving at the deepest root level.

This is a clear indication of the benefits of detachment. To a lot of English speakers, the word detachment sounds like devastation. It has a negative connotation, like letting go of something precious. Actually, though, detachment does not mean letting go of anything healthy, good, or beneficial. Buddhas and bodhisattvas are not going to encourage you to do that. They don't ask you to let go of wisdom, compassion, loving-kindness, or any other positive quality. Detachment refers to what's unhealthy, to what's not good, full of problems. Anything that brings suffering and pain upon yourself—detach and let go of it. Intelligence has the capacity to foresee the difficulties. Only the wisdom that gains insight into the unhealthiness of any given situation can detach from it. You are trying to train to connect with that intelligence, rather than being hooked by habit. Detachment is the practice of a deeper level of intelligence, instead of being hooked by habitual temptation. It's never simply suppression.

If your objective goal is to continue in the samsaric world, to be the same samsaric being you have always been, then training in the spiritual path, in wisdom and skillful means, is useless. You can simply continue to live in samsara, be the same samsaric person you've always been, and never worry about needing anything more. But if you want to be free from samsara, then all these teachings become very pertinent. When practiced, they have tremendous and significant potential to change and transform your mind, because they give us the insight and skillful means to apply our mind to itself.

If we are full of attachment, we cannot actually successfully meditate and calm our mind. We cannot actually enjoy our deeper level of sanity, realize the absolute truth, and gain the eye of the Dharma. We are of little benefit to others and ourselves. That's why detachment practices are very important. We must train in *shamatha*, calm abiding meditation, in order to give birth to *vipashyana*, clear seeing. *Vipashyana* eradicates the ignorance that exists in our mind in the form of the afflicting emotions.

First we must cultivate calm abiding. To cultivate calm abiding, we must practice detachment and have the inspiration to be free of passion. Once again, in English, "free of passion" sounds like a dead log, an inanimate thing. But that's not what it means. To be free of passion means to be free of all disturbances caused by the subtle levels of lust manifesting uncontrollably in our minds. This is what we need to have great passion towards. If we think of passion as enthusiasm, as motivation, as inspiration, then we can have a great passion for detachment. Without that kind of great passion, we cannot overcome lust and craving.

Never learning a lesson is the ego's problem, because ego is in control of habit, not wisdom itself. The Buddha's teaching is a revolution against the ego. The best way to cultivate the passion to be free of attachment is in a retreat situation. In retreat, you can overcome the distractions and all their hindrances and fears. You can abandon all subtle and gross thoughts that make you vulnerable to being hooked by the samsaric lifestyle. Samsaric temptations, samsaric activities hook you—if you are there to be hooked. If you are not there, samsara will not hook you.

People say, "I feel so isolated. I feel so lonely." The lonely feeling is because of wanting somebody to be cozy with, to talk to, and to have fun with. When you have somebody, he or she is a distraction for you. He or she makes you feel like you are part of society, or a family, or whatever.

Think this through: Okay, you don't feel lonely, but is it a good thing to be distracted all the time, to fight, to bicker, always having this dynamic of "You said this," "I said that?" Is it that beneficial to watch somebody's face turn blue, yellow, white, black, along with your mind and your emotions turning blue, white, yellow as well, going up and down on an emotional roller coaster a hundred times a day with someone else? Not only do you have to deal with your own karma, you also have to deal with somebody else's karma. Contemplate. With this person, you're not lonely, but is that good, is it blissful? [*Laughs*] What makes the wrinkles appear on your face so fast? What makes your brightness disappear? What makes your hair gray and your youth vanish? Practitioners have to be objective. It's not a matter of judgment. Being objective is determining whether a thing is pleasant or not. Is it true happiness? It is real bliss? Is it anything other than suffering?

The point is to develop weariness, a realization of samsara as samsara, of samsara as suffering, and a desire to not be in it forever. We need detachment from samsara, and thus also inspiration to get out of it. Weariness is different from depression in that weariness has a sense of determination to get over it. Depression wants to dwell in the state. Weariness has a very hopeful state inside of it. The more weariness you have, the greater the hope. Depression is not hopeful. Milarepa had the greatest weariness, the most hopefulness for himself, and he got enlightened.

Weariness recognizes the cause and conditions and sees the way out. Even though you enjoy relationships, ultimately everything is impermanent. How can you sincerely be attached to something that you know is impermanent and going to change? If you see how in the next moment something is impermanent and gone, but in that previous moment you allowed yourself to be attached, you are a little foolish. Because you know how painful it is to have that attachment and then to lose what you're attached to. Attachment is the machine that makes the pain.

When we're attached, it's obvious. Attachment is projected from inside out onto the object. Not recognizing samsara as full of suffering, we project samsara to be bliss. Samsara is impermanent; we project it to be permanent. Samsara is full of filth; we project it to be pure. Samsara has no reality; we project reality onto it. Projections never exist in the absolute. Even in the relative they are absolutely contrary to what is true. If we empower attachment, we will never see the truth in either the relative or the absolute sense. We will not experience emptiness, understand impermanence, or see the impurity of samsara and its suffering. Our mind will be bound to grasping.

Of course, realization of the absolute truth is best, but even understanding according to the relative is extremely beneficial. When wisdom dawns, you use the absolute to overcome any neurosis. But prior to that, you have to use relative reasoning. For instance, when you see the object of your attachment as a source of bliss, as pure, as permanent, as a real thing, engaging in intellectual reasoning helps you determine that the other person is not the source of bliss, is not pure, permanent, or truly existing. When you see that even in the relative sense, you can overcome attachment and calm your mind.

Absolute truth transcends all duality. The first method prevents attachment; the second one uproots it. You have to practice the first to get the second. In conventional attached mind, the object is always perceived as blissful, permanent, pure, and real. The relative truth is the opposite of that. Absolute truth sees both as a non-duality. That is how the bodhisattva in the *bhumis* experiences. In order for one to get to the *bhumis*, the bodhisattva first has to cross the bridge of seeing relative truth as it is. This is the way to train in overcoming attachment, and this is the practice being introduced. If you do not see the relative truth as it is, then your mind is not going to be calm and at ease.

However much we indulge in attachment, it is like drinking salt water to quench our thirst. Salt water only makes us thirstier. The more we indulge in attachment, the deeper it grows. It makes us want more and more. There's no contentment or satisfaction in it. That's how desire works. The more we indulge, the more we suffer.

Now if you are attached to a person and want all those romantic things to soothe your mind—wanting someone to be cozy with, to comfort you, to be sweet and kind and affectionate to you—all those romantic longings seem simple to have. But in actuality, it never turns out that way. That romantic longing must be checked, examined, and gotten rid of from deep inside. Otherwise you might be either disappointed by the world or hard on yourself, thinking that there is something wrong with you. Either case is not going to be pleasant. It is not possible for those romantic desires to be fulfilled, because beings aren't that simple. You can't program the other being to be that way. Beings come in a full package. You can't marry what you want. You have to marry the full package [*Laughs*]. Any questions?

Student: You said that detachment should be towards unwholesome things, not towards wholesome things. A person who doesn't know anything about Buddhism might say, "Well, if Buddhism is talking about letting go of attachment and desires, than how do you justify the desire for enlightenment?"

Rinpoche: Yeah, that's a very good question. The desire for enlightenment is a desire. But that desire eliminates unhealthy desire. You cultivate and keep it until you transcend it. In the end you transcend it too, because it is a desire.

Student: I understand that I am cultivating egolessness for the benefit of all beings, but what about dedicating merit? There is a density about my conscious negative activity that seems like it would chip away at the savings account I have. I'm afraid I'm making little withdrawals that the negative activity done with such consciousness on my part will somehow take away from the savings that I have accumulated.

Rinpoche: No, it doesn't work like that. The dedication of merit is for you to dedicate whatever merit there is for the benefit of all sentient beings' enlightenment, or for you yourself to be enlightened for the benefit of all sentient beings' enlightenment. That is already designated: It's already put into that account, and nothing can touch that.

Student: So I can't touch it?

Rinpoche: No, you can't touch it. Your wrongdoings can't touch it. It stays there until the designated effect is produced. That's why it's so important to dedicate, because as ordinary beings it's very difficult for us to not get angry. We can't help engaging in aggression sometimes. If aggression could destroy all that long-term accumulated merit, we wouldn't have any merit. Therefore dedication is very important.

Student: Does that mean it's not lost because other people are benefiting from it?

Rinpoche: It's because you have designated it, and thus you have released your own grasp on it.

Student: But then, if you are continuing to do negative activities consciously, then that's eating away at some merit, other merit. You're not accumulating anymore.

Rinpoche: Merit that has not been dedicated will be affected. It's not only that you have released the merit, it's that you've designated it. Until that designated effect is produced, it's not going to go away.

Do you all see the problem of desire from the point of view of the Buddhist teachings? Do you see how the subtle levels become a whole world, and how that becomes a preoccupation with only this lifetime? Do you understand the need for intelligence to see through problems and the downside of things, and do you agree that mind has to reach a level of its own intelligence that outranks the ignorance?

Student: Uproots?

Rinpoche: No, it outweighs, overrides the ignorance that doesn't see the problem and the suffering. That is relative mind, working with relative thoughts. Desire can be overcome by intelligence through the relative mind. It digs deep into its intelligence and finds sanity. This is not suppression; it's actually an antidote. Detachment is both a restraint and a remedy.

Student: What do we do if we realize the problem, but we still give in to it because we haven't understood how strong the problem is?

Rinpoche: As I was saying the other day, first you work with the confusion. Once you have overcome the confusion, then you deal with the habit. Once you work with the confusion and overcome it, then dealing with the habit is much easier. Sometimes it can be fun.

Student: What about the kind of attachment that's positive, like the devotion that's not so much wanting to be cozy with someone but to make someone cozy also, like in marriage or parenting? It seems like you'll always have real loss there. I mean, otherwise you would have to rise completely out of human life.

Rinpoche: [*Laughs*] No, I think it's the degree we are talking about. In those kinds of relationships perhaps there is a subtle level of craving. Let me put it this way: In the case of devotion, there is a feeling of respect, right? Respect for the person who has realization, and admiration of that person's realization and renunciation. You want that level of realization and renunciation for yourself. You devote yourself to hearing the Dharma, contemplating, and meditating, all linked to the teacher. There is a little bit of craving in the beginning. But as it moves forward and you obtain the realization, it actually stops being a duality. You don't crave anything outside—you find the guru, the realization, everything, inside.

Student: Is it also possible for people to be devoted to children?

Rinpoche: With marriage and children, that is questionable. There is attachment there, because marriage and parenting function according to expectations. There are the general expectations of loyalty, hopes and fears, ups and downs, worries, stress, anxieties—all taken as signs of love. These will not arise unless there is attachment. In each case, whether one is a spouse or a parent, there are responsibilities to fulfill in those relationships.

What are those responsibilities in a positive sense? They involve being caring, loving, kind, compassionate, understanding, spacious, and nonjudgmental. I don't know whether attachment comes in any way to assist those things. It is possible that those responsibilities are fulfilled without attachment. You know, a great many realized beings have been married and had children, and their minds were not consumed by attachment.

Student: What about these imprints that are left on our mind from cravings? There are probably a lot of them that we don't even know we left there and we will only find out about when the karmic seeds burst. Is there a way for us to detect them? If we don't realize they're there, how can we apply critical intelligence?

Rinpoche: No, I think you can have some critical intelligence through the hearing and contemplative wisdoms. Use this critical intelligence to examine your own experience. When you identify such things, you apply the remedy. There are also pointers. Suffering is always a pointer. When you are suffering, you can always trace it to one of the five negative afflicting emotions. If you trace it further, you can track it back to coming either from the cherishing or protecting tendency. Tracing even further back, it will be because of holding on to the self, to self-importance. At that point, you can clearly understand what confused act came from the emotions and what emotion was provoked by a particular tendency. Then, simply release yourself from ignorance. It's helpful to do this after the fact as well, because doing it later is purification.

Student: What about the dormant seeds?

Rinpoche: The dormant seeds are not going to be purified right now. You can only purify what comes to the surface and eliminate them. Dormant seeds are purified when you realize emptiness as a direct experience. That's when they are purified as well as eliminated.

Student: If you've given up desire, I imagine you have a lot of boredom.

Rinpoche: See, that's your projection [*Laughs*].

Student: What's the Buddhist remedy for boredom?

Rinpoche: If you study boredom, it comes from having nothing to do that is deeply engaging from inside your own inspired heart. When you are free of all passion, your mind will be sustained at the deepest level of peace and bliss and all the intelligence is at your disposal without any hindrance. Any wisdom that you have will be very agile, in order to actually serve you. One is never going to be bored. Boredom is actually a state of unfulfilled desire, of blocked craving.

Daily Medicine

I WOULD LIKE TO REQUEST all readers to generate *bodhichitta* before reading this next section of teachings. To generate *bodhichitta* is to wish to attain enlightenment for the benefit of all beings. Whatever you do, whether it's studying the teachings or offering a single butter lamp, if you do it from pure intention, the wish to be enlightened for the benefit of all beings, it will be quite powerful. Intention is very important. Have pure intention within yourself.

The story of Geshe Ben illustrates this. One day a patron was coming to visit him. Geshe Ben was making nice offerings on the altar, and he noticed he was putting extra effort into making these offerings so that his patron would be impressed. As soon as he realized this, he said to himself, "Old monk, don't be so foolish." Instead of continuing, he threw a handful of dust on the altar. Later, the great Indian master Padampa Sangye heard this story and said that Geshe Ben's handful of dust was a better offering than any other offering. Not that the dust is better or worse, but Geshe Ben was working to make his intention pure.

It is important to make your intention pure. Until your intention is pure, do not act. When the intention is pure, act. This is concerning oneself.

At other times it is very important to make your intention clear to others, so that there is no misunderstanding. People can't read your mind, so they guess and create projections.

I suggest that sometimes you contemplate whether it is important to keep the intention inside and simply make it pure, acting from that pure intention. Other times, if that is not enough, state your intention and have it clearly understood.

I am trying primarily to emphasize the aspiration *bodhichitta*. Keep it very pure, and practice loving-kindness, compassion, sympathetic joy, and equanimity so that all beings, including yourself, can overcome their self-importance. This self-importance is the root of all suffering. So, insofar as you are able, prevail over it. Instead of holding on to these atoms as a body, or these countless moments of awareness as a self, see how there is no self to be found in these heaps of particles or in these moments of awareness. The self is nothing other than the projection of ignorant mind. Realize the view of egolessness, convincing yourself of the truth that all beings desire happiness and freedom from suffering. Hold whoever has a mind as the cherished self, and generate the intention to treasure and protect them as you would yourself.

From that foundation, generate the feeling to bring all these beings into relative and ultimate happiness—relative happiness being to experience whatever wholesome happiness there is in samsara, and ultimate happiness being enlightenment itself. Similarly, work to bring them out of suffering, both relatively and ultimately. Relatively, try to free them from the sufferings of the lower realms and bring them to the higher realms. Ultimately, try to free them completely from the sufferings of samsara. Have this wish for all beings' enlightenment constantly in your mind.

Understand that to successfully bring all beings to enlightenment, you first must get enlightened yourself. Engender this aspiration *bodhichitta* to be enlightened for the sake of all beings, without the tiniest trace of self-centeredness in your heart. Work on this all the time so that it becomes genuine. This you can do practicing on your cushion. This wish is the seed of wisdom. It is even the beginning of the realization of egolessness as well.

After that, do the practice of the six *paramitas*. Do a generosity practice daily, such as *Riwo Sangcho*, which is incense you burn for the beings of different realms as a food offering. Maybe do a small *tsur*, a burnt food offering that gives food to hungry ghosts. There is also the practice of giving water to them. Any small generosity practice is beneficial, especially in the summer, when you can save the lives of flies and bugs you see drowning.

Always try to restrain yourself from selfish thoughts and the five afflicting negative emotions. Practice *bodhichitta* and virtuous deeds as much as possible. Offer the benefit to others by dedicating the merit to them. This can be a discipline applied to daily practice.

Working with your anger, short temper, and tendency to overreact, transform them through the practice of patience. When you react aggressively, for the most part, you yourself are hurt in some way. Be with that raw hurt for a moment and see that is not such a big deal and that you don't have to react according to your habitual pattern. Either generate compassion to overcome the anger, or appreciate the opportunity to be patient. Do the patience practice in this way.

Always apply your three allies: the ally of inspiration, the stable ally of self-confidence, and the ally of retreat. With mindfulness and vigilant practice, engage yourself in virtue. With a delightful attitude make yourself agile in applying yourself to practicing with everything that arises.

Meditate with detachment regarding all outer things. Train in seeing yourself and others as equal, and exchange yourself with others. Try to meditate a little bit on the egolessness of the self and the egolessness of dharmas.

The path of enlightenment is right here on a daily basis. If you study this text of *The Way of the Bodhisattva*[5] alone, it becomes very clear. You can transform and change your life in small ways. For example, the perfection of generosity is not that you have eliminated all beggars from the world. It's when you have a mind that is absolutely free of attachments and is willing to give. That is the perfection of generosity. Even if you cannot do it in real life, being able to do something like that in your mind, like the practice of *chod,* where you visualize giving away your body, has equal merit. Similarly, the perfection of discipline is not that no one is ever harmed in the world, or that you somehow secure everyone's happiness. It's that you have the deep conviction to avoid hurting others and the objective of restraining yourself from harming others. These practices are all in the mind, not out there. In the West there is this thinking about doing something big and showing it to the world in a way that proves your existence, your worth. If it is inside, it's not considered so important because it's not something that you are able to show to others. In many ways that kind of mind-set is often caught up in self-importance. It's not going to be so helpful.

Our discussion currently falls on the point where *bodhichitta* has already been born and secured. In the meditation chapter, I taught on how to abandon the distractions and the thoughts of the distractions, and then the meditation, *samten,* on *bodhichitta.*

The real meditation of *bodhichitta* here involves equalizing one-self and others and then exchanging oneself and others. We are in the section on exchanging oneself and others.

First, there is the practice of exchanging yourself with some-one considered to be lower than you and who is envious of you. You overcome your own pride by practicing jealousy. If you have good intention, even the negative emotions can be applied as a remedy. There's nothing intrinsic in the negative emotions. They can be overcome by positive intention. Next, if you have com-petitive feelings with people equal or a little bit higher than you, then you exchange and overcome the feeling of competitiveness by taking others to be yourself.

After this, exchange yourself with someone who looks down on you, who is arrogant. You can read the traditional language for this in *The Way of the Bodhisattva*. Here, I will paraphrase a bit. Exchange yourself with someone who acts very arrogantly towards you. Mentally enact this so that you are the other person and that person is you, so you have the ability to go with it more strongly. Think in this way:

> How dare this pathetic person compete with me? People say that he does. He has no way to be equal with me. He lacks the hearing wisdom, the intelligence, and the qualities of nobility in his physique, and also my class and wealth. Without any way in which to compare himself to me, how could he ever think he could do so? My qualities are renowned. I will make sure that all who are devoted to me will have a tremendous amount of delight in seeing me. Just hearing my name, everyone will exclaim ooh and aah! I will remain in the pleasure of fame and name. If he

behaves, I will allow him to have a little bit of whatever respect or wealth he gets. If he works for me, I will allow him to have his tiny pleasures. Otherwise I'll take even that away from him. I will bring ruin to him and all the misfortune he dreads. If you ask me why I am so mean to him, it's because I know for how many lifetimes he has done wrong to me.

Here, "I" and "other" have become opposite; you've exchanged self for other. You are the arrogant one, and the other person is in your place. On an inner level, you are talking to your ego. From here, switch back to normal self reflection. Here's how that goes:

This mind of the ego actually desired to be happy, but not knowing how to apply itself and thus being self-centered, it has done everything wrong, trying to work for the benefit of the self-centered one. Through this mistake, I have experienced nothing other than suffering. Through these countless aeons of immense struggle, I have not accomplished any happiness. All the suffering and the misery that I dreaded had to be experienced.

Now, entering into this wisdom of *bodhichitta* practice, the altruistic practice of benefiting others, you will see its benefits by yourself. It is in accordance with the teachings of the Buddha, because the word of the Tathagatha will always stand as true and not deceive you. If you had acted like this in the past, by now you would have attained enlightenment. You would not remain in samsara, in the conditions you are now experiencing. If you practice like this—holding all beings as yourself and working for the benefit of others—you will succeed.

All the things that you actually wanted for yourself in the past, for this body, for this life, simply steal it from yourself. Wanting so much for yourself, as you have in the past—for this body, for this life—simply steals happiness away from you. Like Milarepa said, "Dig out the sweet from your own mouth, and give it to others." Even though the sweet is in your possession, if you see somebody who wants it, give it. Whatever the challenges and the difficulties may be, be generous in acting on the behalf of others. For instance, if you have trouble giving one dollar, give five dollars instead. Do the action you've avoided even more intensely, so that your initial impulse becomes insignificant.

"If you are happy, others are sad; if you are high and mighty, others are low."[6] In the old days, you would have been satisfied, content, and happy with this situation. This time, do not be happy and content. This time try to put others in your place, while you compete against yourself. For instance, if you are put on a higher seat and somebody is unhappy in the lower place, do not be happy sitting higher. Have the other person sit higher, while you take the lower seat. Or, if somebody is unhappy because you've gotten an acknowledgment that others have not, don't be happy with that situation. Give the acknowledgment to the other person. Act as if you are competing against yourself. This cuts off the whole dynamic and also cuts off your arrogance and competitiveness, as well as the tendency towards jealousy from both your side and the other's side.

Take on others' misfortunes in any way you can and exchange them with what you yourself have as a pleasure. When you're not doing that, look at your mind, how it is getting more spoiled, more lazy, less committed to working with the greatest intention that you can work with, and also recall the joy that could be gained from doing that. Always examine your own faults, even if a situation is somehow not your fault. By being able to take the blame on yourself you can cover somebody's mistakes. Do that, because there is much delight and benefit for others to be found in that. From the ego's mind there's none, of course, but from the point of view of altruistic mind, there most definitely is.

Don't hide anything you've done that might make you seem like a fool. Confess it first to the Three Jewels, and then, as you gain strength, confess to people you are close to. When you feel even stronger, confess to strangers. Eventually you can confess to enemies or people who would take pleasure in hearing about your mistakes. Don't be concerned about how much satisfaction they get out of your impropriety. This is a way to increase your strength. When you admit what you did wrong to somebody and take all the blame, often they change their position, and that changes the relationship. If not, you have nothing to lose, because you've gained the strength inside yourself.

Give all fame to others, just like the wind carrying it away and spreading it everywhere. To override any sense of special attention, personal glory, or your own importance, pray to have the attention go towards someone else. Be a really good worker who doesn't need to be noticed but works for the benefit of beings. Always conceal your positive characteristics and praise others' smallest, tiniest qualities. Hide others' downfalls, or at least don't let them bother you.

However much you've done wrong to others in the past, being carried away by the force of ego in all sorts of ways, turn that situation around and try to do good to others. Deprive the ego of the leisure and privilege of doing things solely for the self. In this way, restoration happens: Karmic debts are paid, and the problems that are the fruit of karmic debts are also purified. If you've done wrong to someone you dislike and you then do the opposite, slowly, slowly there will be a natural change. Keep your own ego tamed, like a new bride entering into a big and powerful family. A new bride will always be shy and timid. Always keep your ego in that way. Do not let pride and arrogance fill up inside you.

Let the discipline of these instructions truly affect you. Be your own disciplinarian. In monasteries they have a disciplinarian. You need to be your own disciplinarian. If you behave, leave it alone and simply be good. If you find you're not behaving, apply wisdom and skillful means to yourself. When your mind doesn't behave or wants to act according to old habits in an egotistical way, have this internal dialogue with yourself:

You have destroyed me in the past. Now it is not going to be so easy. Previously, I was gullible and vulnerable; I just had you to guide me. Now, I see what your trickeries are. I see how you have harmed me. I see where you would lead me, and the results that would come from following you. Prior to this I had no wisdom. Now, with the wisdom of the *Way of the Bodhisattva*, I'm not going to be so easy to fool.

Make sure your self-confidence in the practice stays stable. Abandon whatever feelings of loyalty to the ego you may have. Being loyal to the ego is not going to bring any positive result. Loyalty binds us to the suffering that the ego creates. Any kind of defensiveness comes on behalf of the ego. Deeply understand that this is not a proper thing to support or to defend. Loyalty to the ego will result in nothing other than ruin.

Always think that you have completely sold yourself for the benefit of beings. Bring this to mind at all times. When eating, when dressing, when receiving a salary or a gift, always think that it was given by mother sentient beings. In terms of work, do not think that you are working for a particular company, but for the benefit of all sentient beings. Do not particularly identify that you are living in Palo Alto and working in Silicon Valley. Rather, think that you are working for the larger benefit of all beings. Breaking down those reference points and broadening them shrinks the ego. Since you have reaped many benefits from the practice of altruism and sold yourself completely to the benefit of mother sentient beings, don't complain.

Scold the ego in the following way:

You have brought me to the lower realms. You are like a prison guard shifting me from one prison cell to another. You have handed me to the *yamas,* the lords of the lower realms, countless times. I have suffered so long due to intoxication with you. I now see this very clearly. Now that I am not intoxicated, I can remember what has happened. I have all these intelligent grudges against you.

In this way, conquer all selfish thoughts.
Any questions?

Student: I am still working to understand the birth of ego. We have the absolute mind and the relative mind. The relative mind comes out of the *bardo*. The five sense consciousnesses come into being, the organs develop, and somewhere along the line the thinking consciousness connects all these. We are born and have the notion of self and other. Is thinking consciousness the birth of our ego?

Rinpoche: The thinking consciousness has been there all along. Once it has entered into the combined egg and sperm, from that point on it is conditioned, all the way until the brain develops. Its development is in relation to this world. When our consciousness enters into the womb, it sees a father and mother in union. There are countless *bardo* beings trying to find a body, competing for the possibility of birth. That is their whole purpose. Due to the consciousness's previous karma with the mother and father, an individual is conceived. When it's a boy, there is attachment to the mother and aggression towards the father. If it's a girl, there is attachment to the father and aggression towards the mother. So, there is something to what Freud said [*Laughs*]. Nowadays it's become clearer. Mother and daughter relationships are intense, and so are father and son relationships. This all begins at the time of conception.

It also depends on where the thinking consciousness comes from. If it was from the human realm, there are human thoughts. From a realm like the animal realm, there are thoughts, but mainly with images not with words. When the consciousness enters the combined sperm and egg, it has not yet developed into a full body and become conditioned to the new form. The ego does not exist only from this point on. This feeling has existed for countless lifetimes. Prior to reentering this world, the consciousness holds on to the mental body, known as the illusory body, as the self. This mental body is like the body you have when you travel in a dream, but your physical body is not traveling. You have an image of the physical body traveling. Similarly, in the *bardo* you mainly have an image of your previous birth, and you are traveling with that. You hold on to the self in that way.

Student: By cutting these ego strings, we're cutting them not only from this lifetime, but all lifetimes?

Rinpoche: All lifetimes. You can't perceive a snake if there is no rope, right? Ego is based on the *skandhas,* the aggregates. The aggregates are like the rope that actually makes you believe that there is an ego, a snake. You find out that there is no ego, no snake, by the process of questioning. Is there actually an ego with the characteristics of being singular, permanent, and intrinsic—meaning something that exists by itself without causes and conditions? You will not find anything in the *skandhas* like that. Hence, you will be able to prove the opposite of what we hold the self to be.

Student: I just have one question about exchanging self and others. How can we avoid projecting onto somebody else what we *think* they are feeling? For example, let's say I have a funny exchange with someone, and I think, "Oh, he's jealous of my accomplishments." Then I exchange self and others, and I try to imagine everything I am supposed to. But what if he really wasn't feeling jealousy?

Rinpoche: It could happen like that. But I think the point here is that there is never anything other to do than to clear up what's going on in your mind. The whole point is to clean up your mind. If you think somebody is jealous and behaving enviously, you react to that. This practice of exchange cleans up your own mind, right? You are not going to perpetuate that dynamic and cause suffering.

Student: I was having a conversation with someone last night about Westerners and how we feel really hurt, how there's a lot of pain. We have so many wounds, you know? And there is this feeling that there is so much I have to work through and that I have to heal. I was wondering how much healing should really be going on. How much should I be worried about healing, or is that just an ego trip? Should you just cut through? But at the same time, how much ego comfort do you need before you can destroy it? How much do you have to stroke yourself before you can say, "Okay, I'm done!"

Rinpoche: [*Laughs*] That's a very good question, actually. You know a lot of people in psychology have this idea that you need to have a healthy ego. You need to have some ego before you destroy it. They always say that. I'm sure they have a point. But for instance, someone who has a problem with low self-esteem is not lacking an ego, at least not from the Buddhist point of view. Whenever you think, "I'm lacking this, I'm lacking that; I don't have this, I don't have that; I'm this way, I'm that way," you are all the while holding on to a sense of "I" very strongly. It's true that in the West people pay a lot of attention to mind, and particularly to their feelings. When you pay too much attention to ego ruling your mind or feelings, you become hypersensitive, and there is never a break from the pain.

In the mind stream of someone who pays so much attention to their own feelings, there is not any realization of egolessness or of being able to moderate their ego's workings. Such a person becomes hurt much more easily. They begin to have a very thin skin. Even if they originally had thicker skin, it becomes thinner. Paying attention to your mind with some degree of wisdom is always important. Otherwise, people who meditate can become much more sensitive and reactive. Sometimes they are even worse than normal people, because they have thinner skin. This is because their meditation is not guided by wisdom. They're merely watching their feelings and their thoughts, that's all. We need to be guided by the wisdom of Dharma.

Student: It seems like, if you had conditions as a child or even as a grown-up where you were harmed and you have hatred and aggression towards yourself, you can talk to the ego at the same time as working with that—that you can address both of them.

Rinpoche: Yeah, at the same time that is the support. It's hard to chew, but the teachings on karma are very helpful. Like, for instance, the fact that someone has done nothing bad in this life doesn't mean that others don't hurt him or her. There are many cases of children and adults being harmed and wronged by others when they have done nothing. If you don't accept karma, then things can become very difficult. When you have done nothing but have been greatly wronged and harmed, the justification for anger, resentment, and holding a grudge can be very deep. But the harm has to have come from previous lifetimes, from some negative karma.

For people who don't believe in previous lives, this situation becomes harder. But for the people who believe in past lives and karma, it becomes easier to see how maybe this is not a result of this life's negative action, but of a previous lifetime. Look how much damage we do to beings. Every day we slaughter animals who have not done the tiniest bit of harm to us. From this perspective, if we accept karma, a lot of those old wounds that we cannot justify other than as the result of somebody being mean to us can be seen as the result of previous karma we are unaware of. From this perspective, it's easier to forgive. And the forgiveness heals our heart, right?

Student: I was going to say that when you have a traumatic experience, it seems to me you can go either way: Follow your ego and never heal yourself, or choose to work with the feelings that come up, the ones that you talked about, the anger and guilt, and sort of sit in the fire with those. So is that burning up?

Rinpoche: That is the burning up of the karma. Moreover, when you get to the other side, to the forgiveness and the reasons for forgiveness, you are able to heal your mind from within. That inner healing is the most effective burning of past karma. You are right: When somebody has those kinds of tragedies in his or her life, it's not easy to immediately do these practices. Their brains and mental patterns have been shaped by that trauma. But if one sees the wisdom of working with it skillfully, that is the seed of liberation. Slowly, slowly with a can-do, rather than a "can't-do" attitude, if one works with this, that seed will blossom. That can be the encouragement, and also the path to freedom. However, it's not always possible to do that. Sometimes there is not the seed to do so.

Student: I understand the karma of harming someone, and then getting it back. What about natural disasters?

Rinpoche: Natural disasters are also a part of that.

Student: What's the karma of being caught in an earthquake?

Rinpoche: It's not that you have karma with an earthquake. If you read *The Words of My Perfect Teacher,* you will understand how certain karma manifests in the environment. Your past-life karma results in the circumstances of your current environment. Somebody who has harmed a lot of beings in the past may still have the positive karma to be born in this world, but some of the negative karma of having harmed others can manifest as well, by living in a frightening and dangerous environment. There is a karma that results in the environment. Disasters are always part of that. Otherwise, there is no explanation for why certain people experience natural disasters and others don't.

Student: Is there intrinsically good or bad karma, or is it all in how someone responds?

Rinpoche: No, there is no intrinsically good or bad karma. But that doesn't mean that if one goes through an experience of negative karma or positive karma, that karma is burnt up. Maybe a portion of that karma is burnt up. It could be completed at that time, or it could be that one will need to go through the same experience many times. If one responds positively rather than negatively and applies the antidote, perhaps it changes things so that one does not have to go through it in a similar way in the future. Look at it this way: Some animals go through disaster on a daily, monthly, or yearly basis, birth after birth after birth. Going through something one time doesn't mean one has burned up all of a particular karma. Only a portion of the karma is being burned up.

Student: What influence do we have when we share merit?

Rinpoche: How much of your merit somebody can receive depends on your connection with him or her. The ability to influence his or her life is based on karma. If there is karma to benefit them, then it does. If not, mostly what it does is to work on purifying your own karma.

Application

NOW WE WILL ACTUALLY DO *tonglen* practice, the practice of sending and receiving:

Bodhichitta of Aspiration

TO ENGAGE IN this practice, begin with the *bodhichitta* of aspiration. Make the following wish:

> May all sentient beings be the object of my motivation to attain enlightenment; may I single-handedly guide them to liberation and work until the end of time to bring them all to enlightenment.

Aspiration *bodhichitta* is the genuine longing to attain enlightenment for the benefit of all mother sentient beings. It is praying that they may all be free from suffering and attain both relative happiness and the ultimate happiness of enlightenment. Pray over and over again to attain enlightenment for the benefit of all mother sentient beings.

Think,

May I attain enlightenment for the benefit and welfare of all mother sentient beings. May I attain enlightenment so that I can bring all mother sentient beings to enlightenment. May I attain enlightenment so that I can free all mother sentient beings from the suffering they experience in the cycle of existence.

Make this wish very strongly, genuinely, and deeply. Make it an integral part of the beginning, middle, and end of your practice of the Dharma.

Whatever practice you do, do it based on this motivation. In the same way that the intention to travel to Bodh Gaya is formed before you begin the journey, ensure that this intention is always guiding your practice. Make your practice the journey to enlightenment itself.

Equalizing Yourself with Others

NEXT, EQUALIZE YOURSELF with others. Continuing with the practice of aspiration *bodhichitta,* first see all sentient beings as equal to you. Just as you desire happiness, all sentient beings desire happiness. There is no difference whatsoever in any aspect between you and all other sentient beings. You are completely equal to all other sentient beings, in every respect. You are equal in sharing a deep longing and desire for happiness. Just as you desire to be free from suffering, all other sentient beings wish to be free from every aspect of suffering too. There is no difference between you and other sentient beings. You are completely equal to all other sentient beings, and they are completely equal to you.

It is really important for you to realize that there is no difference between you and all other sentient beings. It is also important to implement this essential realization in your life as best as possible in every action. Genuinely believe this; always keep this thought at the front of your mind. Abandon all logic and reasoning that supports your own self-importance and causes you to act selfishly.

Meditate on this, and you will see that you and all other sentient beings are truly equal. You will feel this equality in your heart to the extent that you can express it in everyday life, and you will be able to recognize when it is present or absent from your actions. At this point, you can move on to exchanging yourself and others.

Exchanging Yourself with Others

EXCHANGING YOURSELF with others takes you a step further. Visualize a human being or an animal in tremendous pain. Animals have the same desire to be happy and to be free from suffering that you have. They experience happiness and suffer tremendous pain when others inflict it on them. Imagine a lobster or a crab. Consider this lobster not only as a sentient being but as your own mother. And now this mother sentient being is being boiled alive, plunged into a pan of boiling water. Think that this being has been your mother in countless lives.

How does this make you feel? How your heart goes out towards this sentient being! How incredibly painful it must be for your mother to endure this suffering, which is inflicted on her without her having done any wrong or caused any harm to anyone in her present life. The lobster is boiled, alive. Feel this suffering and pain. See how horrible it is, how terrible it is, that such suffering exists in samsara.

Tonglen

PRACTICE *tonglen* by letting this image create a feeling of compassion within you and using this compassion as your base. Take the suffering upon yourself in your mind in the form of a dark cloud. And then send out your kind and compassionate thoughts and feelings, without any stinginess or hesitation, so that all your merit is shared with this mother sentient being. Believe that this being is liberated from its suffering immediately and has obtained the causes and conditions of enlightenment.

First, practice with just one being as your object. Then think that, just as this being suffers, there are innumerable human and nonhuman beings who are suffering just as much. Whoever you can imagine is going through similar pain, and your heart opens to them, feels compassion, and goes out to them.

Try to take the suffering of all these beings into yourself in the form of a black cloud. Then extend your positive thoughts and emotions, all your merit, to these beings in the form of white light. As the light touches all sentient beings, they are freed from suffering and attain all the causes and conditions of enlightenment.

From time to time, reflect on how resistant you are to opening up, how afraid you are, and how concerned you are for yourself. Realize that this is just your ego protecting itself. In order to attain enlightenment, your ego must gradually dissolve. Therefore, realize that it is extremely important to practice exchanging yourself for others, using your breath as the medium.

Think of the all the suffering in the lower realms, and practice *tonglen.* Think of the suffering of all sentient beings, and practice *tonglen.* As your practice grows stronger and stronger, and you feel able to practice in a way that increases your compassion and opens your heart further, you develop the fearlessness and strength of *bodhichitta* in the core of your heart. Gradually you dissolve your selfishness, your self-protection, and your grasping onto ego.

At the end, rest in the nonconceptual state of mind free of reference point for as long as you can.

Finally, dedicate the merit for the benefit of all mother sentient beings.

FOR NOW, THIS IS just an intellectual practice. To be able to actually do this, you must progress a long way along the *bhumis.* So aspire to make this practice real. There's a story of a master who was teaching, seated on a throne. Somebody nearby hit a dog with a stone, and he actually fell off his throne. People thought he was being really pretentious, until he showed them the bruise on his body that was in the same place that the stone had struck the dog. Many stories like this one show how *tonglen* is practiced along the different *bhumis.* How wonderful it would be if you could do this at some point in the future! For now, work on training your mind, developing *bodhichitta*, and purifying your obscurations.

Move on to considering others more important than yourself. If an action is genuinely being carried out for the benefit and welfare of all sentient beings, you should have no fear or concern for yourself at all, not even about giving up your life. In one of his previous lives, Buddha Shakyamuni was a prince who gave others all that was dear to him: He even gave his body to a starving tiger.

We should admire and applaud such stories of courage, and we should aspire to give birth to the freedom, strength, and fearlessness that arise out of *bodhichitta* and out of considering others to be more important than ourselves. We should aspire to serve sentient beings genuinely, without the slightest regret, concern, fear, or attachment for ourselves. We serve them by placing more emphasis on their enlightenment, their liberation, and their freedom from suffering than on our own. If an action will bring benefit to mother sentient beings, even if it involves going into the depths of hell and enduring that pain for aeons, we should do so without the slightest hesitation, as easily and freely as a swan dives into a lake.

How wonderful it would be to realize our true nature, to bring *bodhichitta* and its magnificent qualities of power, strength, fearlessness, and selflessness to fruition, and to cherish the abandonment of selfishness! We should cherish, praise, and applaud whoever possesses the quality of selflessness, and the genuine strength and fearlessness that arise from selflessness deeply rooted in loving-kindness and compassion. And we ourselves should aspire to such selflessness.

These are all practices based on the advice for generating aspiration *bodhichitta*. Doing this fully is too much for us right now: We can only imagine doing these practices in our mind. But we can exercise our mind by taking the suffering of others onto ourselves, offering them our own well-being, and giving them our own happiness, merit, and everything positive. All these practices can have a tremendously powerful effect on our mind. And as we progress, the possibility of us manifesting as bodhisattvas arises.

Engagement Bodhichitta

TO PRACTICE ENGAGEMENT *bodhichitta,* begin by sitting quietly. First do a little bit of *shamatha* practice, just to calm your mind. Focus on the breath, relax your mind, and then meditate on the meaning of *prajñaparamita.* Recite the words of the *prajñaparamita,* such as the *Heart Sutra,* contemplating and meditating on the words as you do so. If you don't recite the whole *Heart Sutra,* then at least recite the verses praising *prajñaparamita:*

> *Beyond words, beyond thought, beyond description,*
> *   prajñaparamita*
> *Unborn, unceasing, the very essence of space,*
> *Yet it can be experienced as the wisdom of our own rigpa.*
> *Homage to the mother of the buddhas of past, present, and*
> *   future!*
>
> *Prajñaparamita, inexpressible by speech or thought,*
> *Unborn, unceasing, with nature like the sky,*
> *Which can only be experienced by discriminating awareness*
> *   wisdom*
> *Mother of the Victorious Ones of the three times, I praise and*
> *   prostrate to you!*

You could also recite:

> *Form is emptiness; emptiness also is form.*
> *Emptiness is no other than form,*
> *Form is no other than emptiness.*

You can continue with the section that begins, "In the same way, feeling, perception . . ." Repeat the lines in your mind, and then meditate deeply on them. You can do the same with other parts of the *Heart Sutra*, or meditate on the whole sutra. Then, read from Nagarjuna's text *The Root Verses of the Middle Way* (Skt. *Mulamadhyamakakarika*, Tib. *Uma Tsawé Sherab*).

> *Everything that arises interdependently is unceasing and*
>   *unborn,*
> *Neither nonexistent nor everlasting,*
> *Neither coming nor going,*
> *Neither several in meaning, nor with a single meaning.*
> *You, the teacher of peace, who pacifies all complexity,*
> *Completely enlightened Buddha, perfect among human*
>   *beings,*
> *To you I prostrate!*

You can do the same with other verses that speak to you and elucidate the absolute nature. Repeat the lines, and then meditate on their meaning. Then at some point let go of conceptual mind, and rest as best as you can in the nonconceptual state of mind.

At the end, dedicate any merit gained through your actions for the benefit of all mother sentient beings, so that they too may receive this merit:

> May this merit relieve their suffering and ultimately liberate them from the illusions of samsara. May this merit bring them to enlightenment. May they realize their own enlightened nature and obtain all enlightened qualities.

Acknowledgments

THE BEAUTY AND PROFUNDITY of Dzigar Kongtrül Rinpoche's
teachings cried out for a venue, hence *Uncommon Happiness* came
into being. With his inspiring and moving presentation, *The Way
of the Bodhisattva* came to life in an invigorating and practical way.
So, the first expression of gratitude is offered to Rinpoche himself for not giving up on us hopeless beings and guiding us from
his heart. Secondly, without the encouragement of the gifted and
beautiful Elizabeth Mattis-Namgyel, this book would not have
appeared. Thanks to your positive spirit and pure perception.

The list of other people responsible to creating this valuable work include Laura Dainty, transcriber; Kerry Moran, editor; Meghan Howard, copy editor; Joan Olson, typesetter; Zack
Beer, meticulous proofreader; and to Richard Gere and the Gere
Foundation as the production sponsor. Much sincere gratitude is
offered for their efforts and kindness.

Appreciation goes to the Rigpa and Mangala Shri Bhuti
Centers for permission to integrate the guided meditations on
the Four Immeasurables and Tonglen included in the Training
and Application chapters here. These teachings took place at
Dzogchen Beara in Ireland, May 16th and 17th, 2003.

May we apply these instructions in every moment until we fully embody them.

May this be auspicious!

Mangala Shri Bhuti Centers

MANGALA SHRI BHUTI is a nonprofit Tibetan Buddhist organization under the direction of Venerable Dzigar Kongtrul Rinpoche. Mangala Shri Bhuti offers programs on introductory and advanced Buddhist topics by Dzigar Kongtrul Rinpoche and other lineage holders.

If you would like more information on Rinpoche's teaching schedule, or our collection of recorded MP3s available, please visit Mangala Shri Bhuti's website: www.mangalashribhuti.org, or use the contact information below.

In Colorado:
Mangala Shri Bhuti
P.O. Box 4088
Boulder, CO 80306
(303) 459-0184

In Vermont:
Pema Ösel Do Ngak Chöling
Study, Contemplation, and
Meditation Center
322 Eastman Crossroad
Vershire, VT 05079
(802) 333-4521

Notes

1. The ten *bhumis* consist of seven impure *bhumis* and three pure ones. In the first *bhumi,* one practices generosity; in the second, discipline; in the third, patience; in the fourth, diligence; in the fifth, meditation. The sixth involves the practice of wisdom, and in the seventh, one practices skillful means. In these first seven there remains a taint of ego or self-grasping in the post-meditation state. The first seven *bhumis* involve effort, whereas in the last three *bhumis* of aspiration, power, and jnana, there is no effort. "It is automatic pilot to enlightenment, the eleventh *bhumi.*" Dzigar Kongtrül Rinpoche (teaching, Rangjung Yeshe Gomde, Legget California, June 6, 2008). For a detailed study of the *bhumis,* see Chandrakirti. *Introduction to the Middle Way,* Boston: Shambhala Publications, 2002.

2. The five aggregates of form, sensation, conception, karmic formation and sensation.

3. Also called *all-ground,* or *kunzhi* in Tibetan, *alaya* literally means the "foundation of all things," the basis of mind and both pure and impure phenomena. This word has different meanings in different contexts and should be understood accordingly. Sometimes it is synonymous with buddha nature or dharmakaya, the recognition of which is the basis for all pure phenomena; other times, as in the case of the "ignorant all-ground," it refers to a neutral state of dualistic mind that has not been embraced by innate wakefulness and thus is the basis for samsaric experience. Erik Pema Kunsang, *Advice from the Lotus Born.* Hong Kong, Rangjung Yeshe Publications, 2003.

4. See Shantideva, *The Way of the Bodhisattva*. Boston: Shambhala Publications, 1997, pp. 131–2

5. Ibid. p. 133

9 789627 341635